Positive Democracy

POSITIVE

DEMOCRACY

By JAMES FEIBLEMAN

The University of North Carolina Press

CHAPEL HILL

1940

KINGSPORT PRESS, INC.   KINGSPORT, TENNESSEE

FOR PETER

Preface

IT IS WITH GOOD REASON THAT PHILOSOPHERS HAVE BEEN
accused of defending lost causes. From one point of
view, philosophy may be defined as the method of
demonstrating that nothing is ever lost. There is, of
course, to each adventure a mortal part; and the accidents which contribute toward the unique particularity
of anything can never be regained. Democracy as it
existed in Greece will never return; nor indeed is there
any good reason why it should, since it was not entirely
what it ought to have been. The individual elements
are never the saving elements of a situation, and the
saving elements alone are worth saving. Thus it is at a
time when the crisis of democracy is most in evidence
that philosophers come forward in its defense.

Democracy may persist or it may disappear, and in the
event that it disappears it may or may not reappear.
Certainly the decision does not rest with the mumbled
or written words of a few philosophers. Explicit philosophy is a series of professional episodes, whereas implicit
philosophy is a name for the nature of things; and what
is known is fabulously smaller than what has being.
Nevertheless, this much remains true: that democracy,
like all events involving human progress, must be
planned, and the conditions for planned events must

be thoroughly set forth before they can come to pass. Thus the philosophical considerations of democracy are not expected merely to bolster actual governments, though lessons may be learned from them in this regard. Rational consideration can only abstract from concrete situations the saving elements of democracy in order that the latter may be made available whenever and wherever democracy is to be applied again in practice.

With anything actual that has eventually failed it is always logical to assume that the failure was occasioned by faults, but it is equally logical to assume further that there must have been a valid aspect of the thing which was responsible for whatever success was momentarily attained. This valid aspect is what we have been calling the saving elements. Thus for the purposes of philosophy (which are identical with the purposes of the future of actual practice) we want to know what the lessons of the past have been. Philosophy, even the philosophy of politics, is independent of the temporal order, but learns from the past what not to try in the future. For every truth there is infinite alternative error, which renders the truth difficult of discovery. However, with every observation some choice is eliminated; and since among the wilderness of alternatives there are families of choices, more progress is being made than would be noticed by dismally surveying the prospects. After all, something must be left to intuition or insight, since we are not strangers in nature.

The actual democracy which we have had in the recent past and which, to some extent at least, still exists in the present, may be characterized as negative democracy; its cardinal principles rest upon the necessity for the maximum practical abstention of government from interference in individual affairs. Negative democracy becomes an easy prey to those forces opposing it both from within and from without which count upon a more aggressive policy. But positive democracy is possible. It is time for democracy to recognize that peace is something for which it is worth fighting. Liberal democracy, as we have come to know it, was historically founded on struggle, and in the cases of French and American democracies on armed conflict. We must learn to take a more militant attitude toward the preservation of liberalism. We want to live in peace, we want to retain our freedom of expression and action, and we want to have the right to work. But we are fast learning from bitter experience that we can only hope to have these things by being more positive about them. We must be ready to fight. The old negative attitude will no longer prove sufficient, if indeed it ever did; and we can safeguard democracy only by zealous vigilance. In this work it will be shown how our passive attitude toward democracy arose in the past, and what the new active attitude must be if democracy is to be kept alive—or revived—as the principle of actual government.

The thesis underlying the arguments of this book may be stated in the form of a manifesto, somewhat as follows. The view that the current economic struggle both within and without the democracies is certain to end with the supplanting of democracy by either fascism or communism is definitely rejected. It is still possible to retain the democratic form of government. Because of its peculiar historical origins and development, democracy has acquired certain characteristics which have seemed essential to it. Their actual association has led to the common belief that democracy is necessarily nominalistic, irrational, negative, individualistic, liberal, capitalistic, and impractical. These characteristics are in part contradictory; their identification in theory is the result of a confusion of logic with history. But what democracy has been is by no means exhaustive of what it could be, and is certainly not what it ought to be. The separate studies pursued herein will lead to definite conclusions concerning the practical features proper to the goal of democratic politics.

FIRST: Democracy ought to recognize the reality of society as an entity which is composed of real individuals and their goods but which is more than a mere aggregate of such individuals.

SECOND: Democracy ought to be ruled by a majority which in turn acknowledges the higher authority of reason. Thus it ought to be a positive, rational doctrine rather than a negative, irrational affair.

THIRD: Democracy ought to promote the welfare of science as essential to its own self-preservation. But it ought to go no further with its own regulations and restrictions than experience will allow reason to go.

FOURTH: Democracy ought to found itself not upon the preservation of property rights but rather upon the recognition of the necessity for the right relation between properties and citizens. In this new property sense, it cannot tolerate any important division of its citizens along class lines.

FIFTH: Democracy ought to be liberal in allowing freedom of expression and a certain measure of freedom of social action, as a consequence of the recognition of the civil rights of the minority under majority-rule. But it ought to secure to all citizens the right to work as well as the right to speak.

SIXTH: Democracy ought to have as an end the futherance of the welfare of individuals as well as of the whole of society. But the motive of the democratic citizen ought to be the furtherance of the welfare of society as well as of individuals.

Just how these and other conclusions emerge from the rational consideration of actual democratic practice will be made clearer from a reading of the following pages.

A number of the chapters, in somewhat shorter form, have been published as separate essays. My thanks are due to the editors of the following journals for the use of material which originally appeared in their pages: to *Ethics* for Chapter XI; to the *International Journal of Individual Psychology* for Chapter VIII; to the *Marxist Quarterly* for part of Chapter I; to the *Modern Monthly* for Chapter IX; to *The New English Weekly* for part of Chapter XIII under the title of "Peirce's Logical Ethics"; to *Purpose* for part of Chapter III under the title of "The Irrational Origins of Rational Democracy," for Chapter V, and part of Chapter VII under the title of "The Definition of Science"; to *River* for another part of Chapter VII under the title of "The Relation of Logic to Experiment"; and to the *Sociological Review* for Chapter X.

I am indebted to G. P. Putnam's Sons for permission to quote from John Dewey, *Liberalism and Social Action;*

to Harper and Brothers for permission to quote from Alexis Carrel, *Man, the Unknown*; to Norton and Company for permission to quote from Ascoli and Lehmann, *Political and Economic Democracy*; to Henry Holt and Company for permission to quote from John Dewey, *Logic*; to Harcourt, Brace and Company for permission to quote from Huntington Cairns, *Law and the Social Sciences*, and from Morris R. Cohen, *Reason and Nature*; and to the Harvard University Press for quotations from *The Collected Papers of Charles Sanders Peirce*, reprinted by permission of the President and Fellows of Harvard College.

JAMES FEIBLEMAN

New Orleans
October, 1939

Contents

APPENDICES

PART I

TRADITIONAL INFLUENCES

I.

Democracy,

the Bourgeois, and Nominalism

Nominalism and the Bourgeois

THE QUESTION OF WHETHER A POLITICAL DOCTRINE OR the philosophical theory upon which it rests occurs first historically is not an easy one to answer. We seek to discover which one is the occasion of the other, because in this way we hope to approach closer to the understanding of the essential nature of the political doctrine. But although such an inquiry is interesting, it will not tell us exactly what we wish to know. For even a very complete knowledge of all the circumstances surrounding the rise of a thing can impart nothing final about what it may prove to be.

The separation of historical occasion from logical cause is a difficult one for the modern mind to make, but it must be made if either history or causality is to be understood properly. When we turn to an examination of the political doctrine of democracy, we find that the same problem confronts us. Here we want to know how democracy arose and what it came to be, preparatory to

3

further speculation as to what it could be. We know that democracy was the political expression of the bourgeois class, the trading burghers who rose up against the restrictions of the agricultural aristocrats. It is this class which has come to be the vast middle class of the modern world, under whose aegis the democracies have flourished. We know also that the dominant philosophy of this recent period has been that of nominalism. The mediaevalists were realists who believed in the reality of universal truths and ideal goals but who also thought that they knew all that it was necessary to know concerning those truths and goals. Their restrictive version of realism brought about a philosophical revolt which came in the name of nominalism: the belief in the sole reality of physical particulars or things. The rise of the philosophy of nominalism and of the bourgeois were simultaneous events. The analysis of this interrelation will prove of interest to our concern with the peculiar form of modern democracy. The question we shall eventually ask is whether democracy is necessarily nominalistic; but before we come to this question we must put another. Is the philosophical doctrine of nominalism necessarily dependent upon its social origins? A satisfactory reply will have to include the separating out of occasion and cause in this dependence. Since there has been a very interesting paper published on these topics, we may take the examination of it as our starting point, for it raises many relevant issues. Did nominalism arise as an apology of the bourgeois theorists of the seventeenth century? Mr. Edward Conze's contention is that it did.

In a paper on the "Social Origins of Nominalism" he states that "Nominalist philosophy expressed the needs of the economic structure that began to shape itself at that time. In the 17th and 18th century, Nominalism was at the basis of the philosophy of precisely those thinkers who most ardently and clearly fought for the realization of a bourgeois conception of society. Could nominalism from the very start have been an expression of bourgeois mentality? I think that we must come to this conclusion." [1] Before we come to agree with any such conclusion, it may be well to examine the premises and argument upon which it rests.

The thesis of the bourgeois origins of nominalism stated by Mr. Conze contains two presuppositions: (1) that the bourgeois class and the nominalistic doctrine have always occurred together historically, the doctrine being a product of the bourgeois *mentality;* and (2) that the nominalistic doctrine stands in the relation of causal dependence on the bourgeois mentality.

It would, perhaps, be possible to show that the bourgeois class and the nominalistic doctrine have always occurred together historically. The Greek Sophists challenged the Socratic doctrine of the objective and independent reality of the Ideas, in favor of a subjective and psychological argumentative skill, requiring a logic unrelated to the question of abstract reality but more fitted for the gaining of commercial advantage in the law courts and the market place. The Sophists were the earliest known nominalists; from the little we know of them they seem to have been good bourgeois. Porphyry was the author of the *Introduction to the Categories* (of Aristotle), the book which first raised the question of nominalism explicitly. But whether Pyrrho, the Greek sceptic, or Capella, the compiler, or Boethius, who wrote a commentary on Porphyry's *Introduction,* all of whom

[1] *Marxist Quarterly,* I (1937), 115–16.

were nominalists, were themselves members of a bourgeois class has not yet been determined. However, coming down to the eleventh century, Roscellinus, the first important scholastic to hold the nominalistic doctrine, was a Churchman; to demonstrate that he was also bourgeois might be difficult. That the nominalists after Occam were bourgeois may be readily conceded, and it is upon the latter group alone that Conze's historical argument rests.

The question is, however, just what does all this prove? Historical arguments to exhibit the necessity of logical relations cannot be valid, and historical arguments are all that Mr. Conze offers. Things that happen together do not necessarily belong together beyond the occasion in which they occur. To reveal that the nominalist doctrine has always been held historically by members of the bourgeois class is by no means to prove the causal dependence of the former upon the latter. Nominalism is a logical doctrine, to which an individual or group of individuals may subscribe at any time. Even if nominalism has *always* been held by the bourgeois, which has not by any means been shown, this would not prove that it *must* be so held, or that it could not arise or exist without the bourgeois. Conze has rightly noted the close historical association, at least in one period, between the two, but he has not demonstrated them to be inevitably associated. Can they be so demonstrated?

The question involves a closer logical analysis of the definitions of both nominalism and the bourgeois. According to nominalism, universals are fictions of the mind, a proposition which renders particular things ultimate and real, and ideas the mental interpretation of these real things. The bourgeois, as the class emergent between peasant and aristocrat, and finally itself the master, may be described as the trading or mercantile class. Since this class is preoccupied with the exchange of goods with a view to material gain, how logical it is that nominalism should seem to it a better philosophy than any other! The priority of material things and the corresponding unreality of ideas would seem to be the natural belief of a trading class. In any case, the relation of nominalism to the trading class as both occurred in fourteenth century Europe does not involve the admission of causal dependence or of any inevitable and necessary association. There would not be anything contradictory involved in the occurrence of nominalism without the bourgeois, or vice versa.

It does seem, however, that in the rise of the bourgeois in the fourteenth century, nominalism furnished the occasion. Nominalism started within the Church, as a protest against the rigid limitations put upon the discovery of universals by the narrow theological realism. Its effects were not confined to the Church but were far reaching. This revolt, which was conducted by the scholastics themselves, allowed for the establishment of many new beliefs and institutions. It gave a free hand to the early empiricists; it made Protestantism, individualism, liberalism, and democracy, possible. It gave rise to the middle class. Indeed it was the occasion for the beginning of the entire trend which took a firm hold on the succeeding centuries.

Logically and metaphysically, the problem of realism versus nominalism primes class affiliations. Membership in a class may be occasioned by a number of external and accidental factors, but in so far as it is a matter of deliberate and conscious choice, it is determined by interest.

Now interest is predetermined by the belief in what is real, which in turn is the result of surrender to some metaphysics. No one could devote himself wholeheartedly to a lifetime of activity in a field which he did not consider of the utmost importance. It is well-known that every profession is considered by those who practice it to be the hub of civilization. The fact that the middle class arose in Europe when it did, that it became the ruling class, and that it conquered the far corners of the earth, followed upon the acceptance of the prime reality of particulars, and hence of material wealth, as superior to universals, which according to nominalism enjoy, if they are real at all, only a secondary reality. Thus the rise of the European bourgeoisie was occasioned by the change from the realistic to the nominalistic philosophy.

Mr. Conze's thesis, in somewhat modified form, may be accepted. Nominalism and the bourgeois logically are closely identifiable. They have been identified frequently in historical time. But there is no causal necessity about their identification; they may or they may not occur together.

Democracy and the Bourgeois

We have dwelt at some length upon the relation of the philosophy of nominalism to the bourgeois because an understanding of this relation will help us to clarify the philosophical nature of democracy. Democracy, the middle class, and the philosophy of nominalism, as we have them today, were all marked by the same influences. Just as the spread of the acceptance of nominalism as a dominant metaphysics occasioned the rise of the trading class, so democracy was popularized as its political expression. The question which we shall want answered about democracy is much the same as the one we have already asked and attempted to answer in the case of nominalism. Is democracy altogether a product of the bourgeoisie whose interests it was established to serve? Does it stand in the relation of causal dependence upon the bourgeoisie? And then there will be a further question which must follow these: is democracy necessarily nominalistic?

It is certainly a fact that democracy was occasioned in the modern world by the need for political and economic expression on the part of the middle class. Trade expansion was only possible under a system of free trade, and free trade could only be defended under a system of other freedoms. The success of the trading class was hampered by the older political forms, by the traditional ruling classes of nobility and clergy. In a day in which new worlds were being discovered and new continents opened to exploitation, equality of individual opportunity suddenly became an immediate necessity for the development of society to its fullest extent. Thus it is true that democracy, as the defense of the sovereign rights of the individual and hence as the rule of the majority, arose when the need became more and more urgent for the economic requirements of the middle class to assume political form. We may frankly admit that the political doctrine of democracy in its present constitution was occasioned by the rise of the middle class.

But we are not committed by this admission to anything more than the description of one period of European history. Historians insist upon identifying inalienably whatever occurs together; those things which are associated in the past must, they say, always continue to be thought of as associated. To some extent, of course, their position is sound. The unique particularity of historical associations is irrevocable; democracy as it has occurred and the bourgeois as it has occurred, specified *exactly* as we have had them in recent centuries in Europe, must always be thought of equally as occurring together and as belonging to the past. It may be possible that things can occur twice in the same way, but it is highly improbable. Each occurrence differs somewhat from all other occurrences. Thus we may expect the middle class back with us in some future period in history and we may expect democracy, too, but each always in some altered form and one more than likely without the other. Thus although democracy arose upon its latest occasion as the political organ of the middle class, it is not cast in such a rôle necessarily, and may arise again on an altogether different occasion.

The kind of democracy we have had in recent centuries has been to a large extent middle class democracy. We shall note shortly just what this has involved. Meanwhile it is instructive to observe that even in historical time democracy has not always been a product of the middle class. The historical instances of democracy are all too few, and so we are forced to revert for illustration time and again to the same examples. The corrupt democracy of classical Greece allowed for slavery, and functioned as a democracy only for citizens. It could hardly be called an instrument of the middle class. Slaves received the same treatment in Greece as in non-democratic countries. What peculiar monopoly did the democratic form preserve? There exist more or less stable primitive societies, which in their political practice may be described as containing large democratic elements, and which have no trading class at all but whose trading is done by the group as a whole or by all individual members. Perhaps it would be possible to have a democracy as the political expression of some class other than the middle class or even of a classless society.[2] Perhaps, also, it would be possible to have a middle class which sought its justification in some other political philosophy, or a middle class which, having attained power, no longer wished to defend a doctrine allowing so much liberty to the individuals of other classes, or even a middle class which sought power frankly on the basis of class interests without democracy.

Thus there is no absolute necessity about the association of democracy with the middle class. Either may occur without the other. Indeed, the association of democracy with the middle class is feasible only where both are founded upon the nominalistic philosophy. We have already noted that the association of nominalism with the middle class is historical but not necessary, and that the association of democracy with the middle class is likewise historical but not necessary. Now let us see whether the same relationship does not hold also in the case of democracy and nominalism.

Democracy and Nominalism

What meaning is there in the assertion that the kind of democracy we have had has been middle class democracy? The answer is simple when we recall that the middle class philosophy has been that of nominalism. We are indebted to Vico and to Spengler for showing us that the leading activities of given periods of social history are always self-consistent. That this is so follows, as we shall learn in a later chapter of this work,[3] from the im-

[2] In this connection, see Appendix IV.
[3] Chapter VI.

plicit acceptance of a dominant philosophy, with which somehow all activities engaged in and all major doctrines established are always (unknowingly perhaps, but none the less surely) made to agree. Thus since the philosophy of the middle class was that of nominalism and the politics of the middle class was that of democracy, we should expect to find that the philosophy of the politics of democracy was that of nominalism. And indeed this was the case.

Nominalism consists in the belief in the sole reality of physical particulars, and hence in the disbelief in the reality of generalities. *This* orange is real, *that* apple is real, but "fruit" is only a convenient verbal usage, having a secondary reality, if any reality at all. In the instance of democracy, the interpretation of a nominalistic political system was a comparatively easy affair. Nominalistic democracy calls for the equal rights of the individuals composing society chiefly because it does not believe in the reality of society. Individuals are real, but society as the generality inferred from them is not real or has at best only a secondary reality. In either case, the social whole is not allowed by nominalism to be as real as the individuals composing it. Nominalism avers that society is only a term of convenience, verbal shorthand to describe an aggregation of individuals. Political nominalism recognizes in collections of individuals, called societies or states, only an aggregation and never an organization. All social organizations are deemed to be fictions, where the only reality resides in the social entities or individuals composing it. Such is the historical association of democracy with nominalism.

But the association of democracy with nominalism is an historical and not a logical one. There is nothing necessary about it. There can be nominalism in political philosophy without democracy, indeed the present political alternatives to democracy are tainted with it; both fascism and communism contain large nominalistic elements. Conversely, there can be democracy without nominalism. Since nominalism as a complete philosophy is an error, this latter point is of especial interest to us. In a way it constitutes the leading thesis of this work, and we shall attempt here to indicate only the metaphysical interpretation. Later chapters will in one fashion or another return to it as bearing on different facets of democracy which are not so obviously metaphysical.

The cardinal principle of democracy is the retention of state power in the hands of the people, and the consequent rule of the majority. This was laid down, as we have seen, on the basis of the nominalistic origins of democracy because of a disbelief in the reality of social organization and a belief in the sole reality of the individual citizens. It was done also to counteract the previous emphasis on the residence of state power in a single sovereign, a situation which did not allow any considerable power to individual citizens. But we do not eliminate error by substituting one error for another. The individual citizens are entitled to their rights as citizens, and society is entitled to its power as society. There is a sense in which the rights and powers of individual citizens cannot properly be presumed by the state, and a sense in which society as a whole has rights and powers which go beyond those of individual citizens.

The main point to remember here is that democracy as a form of political philosophy can be maintained without the retention of nominalism to give it justification. Political democracy can be supported on a basis which does not deny that the reality of social organization is equal with that of individuals. The difficulty has come about through a confusion of reality with value. Once we deny any distinction between the individual and society on the basis of reality, the nominalistic character of the political philosophy of democracy is lost. But democracy itself need not be lost. We can retain democracy by substituting for reality the criterion of value or worth. Thus there is a level whereon social organization is more valuable than any individual citizen in it; but there is also a level at which each and every individual citizen has value for himself and for the whole of society.

This is the true meaning of democracy: each value is absolutely itself. In the political field as in all others this is an empirical fact which must be taken into account. "The basis of democracy is the common fact of value-experience, as constituting the essential nature of each pulsation of actuality. Everything has some value for itself, for others, and for the whole." [4] Individuals in a social organization may constitute by that organization something over and above themselves, without in any way invalidating their own single and individual claims. Similarly, representative government may amount to something more than those it represents, while still having to take the latter into account. The balance admittedly is a nice one and is very hard to maintain. But then what just evaluation is not? Democracy is nothing more than just evaluation in the political field, where the individual and society are allowed to exercise exactly the worth they bear.

The error of the nominalistic interpretation of democracy comes to the fore when proportional representation,

[4] A. N. Whitehead, Modes of Thought (New York, 1938), p. 151.

which nominalism insists is by itself sufficient to insure
democracy, proves to be no guarantee at all. As Mr.
Laski points out, "both Germany and Spain have pretty
grimly disproved the contention that proportional representation gives security and stability to a democratic regime." [5] Nominalism in its atomic insistence upon individual representation leads to such catastrophes of the
majority as the securing of power by Hitler. But democracy itself is something else. *Democracy is that rule of
the majority wherein the rights of the minority are safe-
guarded.* "The minority must be protected in its rights
from outrage by the majority" [6] not only out of a regard
for constitutional law [7] but because there is some "point,
never capable of precise definition, where a minority will
not submit to the power of the majority." [8] Thus the
founding of democracy upon realistic rather than nominalistic premises is an urgent necessity for the saving of
democracy. When the majority is forced to recognize
the rights of the minority, it is in view of the reality of
the whole of the social organization. Such recognition
is accomplished by the reserving of certain rights and
liberties to the individual and by restricting the government to rule through what is freely acknowledged to be
opinion. A situation which calls for agreement on fundamentals by all those involved does not alter the realistic
character of the recognition of minority rights by the
majority.

Thus we are justified by metaphysics in establishing
the philosophical foundations of democracy on the reality

[5] Harold J. Laski, *Parliamentary Government in England* (London,
1938), p. 78.
[6] *Ibid.*, p. 57.
[7] Which, for example, does not exist in England.
[8] *Ibid.*, p. 109.

of both the individual and the state plus the retention of the values of each on its own proper level. The contention of this work is that democracy started badly in modern times by serving as the instrument of a single social class and thus also by assuming at its foundations an erroneous metaphysics. By dissociating itself from special service to the middle class, by setting out to serve impartially as the political government of all human beings, and also by dissociating itself from nominalism and founding itself on empirical realism, democracy can make the claim to philosophical and political justification which, on account of its historical associations, has been denied it.

We have learned that it is possible, despite the close historical association of democracy with nominalism and the bourgeois, to separate them. Democracy can fairly be considered in abstraction. Since we have no particular guarantee that its associations will continue to be in the future exactly what they have been in the past, it would be well to establish the principles of democracy by themselves in order to be able to recognize them under whatever name or in whatever system of government they may occur, and in order to set them up as a goal for future political striving.

In order to complete the arguments involved in this task, however, there are several relevant questions which must be examined, questions arising out of the fact of the long association of democracy with the trading class and the nominalistic philosophy. We have noted that the chief concern of the trading class has been with tangible material property. In the next chapter, therefore, we shall take notice of what the effect would be upon our notions of property if there were to occur a shift from nominalism to realism; and in Chapter III we shall examine the effect upon democracy of its nominalistic origins, speculating there upon a corresponding shift to realism. Since nominalism is always irrational and realism sometimes rational[9] we shall want to know whether a rational democracy is possible and if so what it could mean.

[9] Realisms are not always rational and seldom remain absolutely so for long periods at a time. For instance, in the early Renaissance the Catholic Church became irrational through its prohibition against the empirical discovery of further universals. Conversely, rationalisms are not always realistic, although they tend to become so. For instance, the rational discipline of mathematics which formerly rested upon an a priori basis is now coming to recognize its fundamentally logical and realistic nature.

2.

Property:

From Substance to Function

The Background of Substance

DURING THE PERIOD IN WHICH MODERN DEMOCRACY WAS founded, nominalism grew to be the leading implicit philosophy. The deductive varieties of this philosophic outcome of the decadent scholasticism of William of Occam and his followers were employed in the Renaissance as weapons to be used against all mediaeval forms. Nominalism is the theory of the sole reality of physical particulars. As such it seemed to call for the superior reality of individual persons and physical possessions, in opposition to the prior claims of the mediaeval classes of status and privilege led by the Crown and the Church. Of course the derivation of all social innovations as inferences from a basic nominalism was rarely direct and seldom conscious; but it was sure. The centuries following the Reformation were devoted to exploring the implications of nominalism in every walk of life. One social conception which was deeply affected by the leading change in philosophy was that of property.

Nominalism is essentially a *substance* philosophy. Another name for the "physical particulars" in which nominalism places its sole reality is "material substances." There is no difference between them. Things enjoying sensible qualities, masses having weight, density and dimensions, such are the reals of this world, says nominalism, and they alone are substantial. And it further maintains that all else is in some way secondary and derived. The metaphysically primary importance of substance has been refuted of late in many ways. Nominalism has been denied by many cogent arguments, for example by G. E. Moore [1] and C. S. Peirce,[2] and nominalism, of course, is the substance philosophy, the "physical particulars" which it holds real being only another name for "substantial things." Substance in this sense has also been abandoned in physics by the change from the theory of the irreducible particle of matter (i.e., substance) to that of emissions of energy at a point.[8] Lastly, substance has been abandoned in logic by the change from the Aristotelian substantive-predicate logic to the modern mathematical logic of relations, symbolic logic.

Returning to the problem of social life under the philosophy of nominalism, we are able to see that its activities have been centered around what was deemed to be substantial in it, and this substance obviously must have

[1] *Philosophical Studies* (London, 1922).

[2] *Collected Papers of Charles Sanders Peirce*, eds. Hartshorne and Weiss (6 vols., Cambridge, 1934).

[8] The philosophy of John Dewey contains realistic elements but is predominantly nominalistic. Yet he is aware that the primary category of substance stands exposed as fallacious in modern physical science. See his *Logic* (New York, 1939), p. 91. On p. 96 he remarks: "The category of substance is the reflection of the conception that *things* exist in stable form in the world—an idea not only familiar to, but basic in, all those common sense beliefs that have not been modified by the impact of modern science."

been thought to consist in human individuals and their property. Nominalism as the theory of the sole reality of physical particulars was bound to feature property as the most obvious instance of what was meant by physical particulars. This, we may note, was exactly what happened. The shift from religious ideals to trading realities brought the focus of attention upon property. Property became the fountain and origin of the meaning of social life and its ownership the dominant note in social relations; as a result "status was replaced by contract as the juridical foundation of society."[4] Thus from the long period of subservience to the mediaeval religious hierarchy in terms of other-worldliness, the modern world emerged with a high regard for this-worldliness in the shape of subservience to the individual ownership of property as the source of human liberty and equality.

It is crucial to the argument that the identification of property with substance was never logically justifiable. For a substance is always understood to have a simple location in time and space.[5] But as philosophers as widely divergent as, for instance, Aquinas[6] and Whitehead[7] agree, a thing is wherever it operates. Now, operation certainly involves affection; therefore a thing is wherever its effects are felt. But property operates wherever its ownership is involved, or through monopoly wherever its ownership brings an onus upon those who are deprived of its use. Thus if property has relations which substance does not have, property cannot be a substance.

[4] Harold J. Laski, The Rise of European Liberalism (London, 1936), p. 11.
[5] Substance is that which stands under a peculiarly local relationship (Augustine, De Trinitate, lib. vii, c.4; Locke, Essay on Human Understanding, Bk. ii, Chap. 23).
[6] Summa Theologica, Q. 8, Art. 1.
[7] A. N. Whitehead, Process and Reality (New York, 1929), p. 352.

With the importance of substance diminished, the absolute understanding of property must be correspondingly abated. But it is noteworthy that even on the old basis the close association of property with substance was never valid.

However this may be, the new allegiance to the individual ownership of property worked very well as the instrument of industrial expansion; it finally emerged, however, in the inequalities and rigidities of finance capitalism. Once the expanding market, upon which the capitalistic monopoly of power tool industrialism was predicated, disappeared, the democracies in which capitalist industrialism had flourished were shaken to their roots. The stationary market tended to give way to the contracting market, thus bringing about a reaction on the part of capitalistic industrialism which has more than shaken democracy—it has in some cases done away with it.

The reaction of the capitalistic industrial system has marked the extreme limits of the application of nominalism. The world has in recent years been groping toward a realism in political philosophy which can agree to equalities of ownership of property without calling for the abandonment of democracy in favor of some form of extreme control. This will involve a new conception of property in terms of the philosophy of realism. One object of this work is to interpret the realistic meaning of property, and to ascertain what new meaning of contract would be a necessary consequence of the interpretation.

Just as the leading conception of nominalism brought about the prominence of the notion of substance, so the leading conception of realism brings about the prominence of the notion of function. Realism consists in the theory of the equal reality of all objects of knowledge.

The very term "reality" loses its usefulness in the new context, since it fails to be discriminatory. In place of the old relations of a primary substance, we now have the substance itself consisting of primary relations. Or in other words, there is no longer any final substance as such: an object having incidental relations with other objects. The object itself consists in its relations with the rest of existence. This leads away from the notion of stubborn things having incidental use, to the notion of stubborn use constituting, incidentally, things.

Now, the uses of a thing are its functions. A thing is what it can do;[8] it is literally composed of its possible uses. Thus a dynamic conception has replaced the static one. In accordance with this new conception, property no longer remains a fixed affair, one whose only activity consists in the sufferance of accidents. Instead, it becomes a function, or a set of functions, whose dynamic potentialities constitute what is essential to it. Of course, the social implications of this change go further than the mere definition of property itself. The aspect of the question in which society is most concerned is the following. When the conception of property is turned over from one of substance to one of function what happens to the notion of contract? In order to give a proper answer to this question it will be necessary first to examine the classic meaning of ownership which prevailed under the notion of property as substance.

Property as Function

We have noted that under the nominalistic conception property was a substance. With the incursion of the

[8] The extreme wing of modern logical positivists would argue that a thing is what it does, but this is a narrower conception and, from its limitations, invalid.

modern conception of private property, ownership, which
was a relation sanctified by the law, began to supersede
the law in importance so that the law itself came to be
dependent upon property. "Possession was originally
protected in order to aid the law of crime and tort; it
came at length to be protected in order to aid the law
of property." [9] How far the new orientation went with
the founders of modern democracy is illustrated in what
has become known as the natural law theory, the conception of the courts "according to which property is a
natural right, superior to all human laws." [10] This legal
theory places property before law in importance, and
therefore founds the law upon property. As Cairns says,
this view was the English view of Coke and Blackstone
and, through these men, became accepted in the United
States.

Such has been the legal form taken by the substance
theory of property. On this theory, ownership through
contract justifies that conception of property which carries with it no mandamus to use but merely the right to
keep others off, to prevent use by others. "When I say
'the land on the water front is my property,' I am saying
that with respect to the land on the water front I have
a claim against other individuals that they keep away
from it." [11] This leaves property in the status of an absolutely private affair, an atomic relation completely at
the discretion of the individual. But as we now know
from experience, this conception does not hold under

[9] Huntington Cairns, *Law and the Social Sciences* (London, 1935),
p. 65. Cairns' notes to this and following references are important.
Although I have drawn heavily on Cairns in this section, he is of course
in no wise responsible for the use made of his work here.
[10] *Ibid.*, pp. 72–73.
[11] *Ibid.*, p. 58.

any and all conditions. It holds for small amounts of property where the owner's use alone is involved; the ownership of clothes, of food, of a dwelling, of an automobile, and so on. In cases of property in amounts where use by the owner is practically mandatory, no other conception, perhaps, would serve any better.

But once the boundaries of use are passed, the conception tends to break down. Under the modern system of industrialism, the accumulation of more than can be consumed is possible, and indeed not infrequently occurs. The result is the bad relations of monopoly capitalism, in which the pretension to individual discretion in affairs of ownership is reduced to an absurdity. Under the contemporary extremes, in which most persons own little or nothing but their labor power, and in which property tends to concentrate in the hands of a comparatively few persons, the truth is factually illustrated that it does matter socially after all what use the individual makes of his own property. Ownership appears in its new capacity as a means of social preventing more baldly than the justification of democracy to the majority will allow. The notion of property which was adequate for a negative conception of government and an expanding economy is discovered to be no longer suitable.

Perhaps the source of the error of the substance theory of property was occasioned by the confusion of the ownership of an impulse with its object. This confusion was detected by Bishop Butler in the eighteenth century. As Joad points out,[12] the object of an impulse is not a thing but a process which that thing may make possible. The

[12] C. E. M. Joad, *Guide to the Philosophy of Morals and Politics* (New York, 1938), p. 187.

object of hunger is not food but eating. It is not substances which are the important things in social relations, but rather functions, and thus substances must be treated socially in their functional aspects. The point is highly relevant to the topic under discussion. For where the functions of substances are not exercised, the social relations of the substance in question go by default. Thus the social test of the functions of a substance is its consumption. It is important to emphasize that consumption and not ownership is the object of necessity for the individual at the level of his social relations.

In order to justify this altered conception legally we do not have to initiate anything strikingly new. It is but necessary to return to the origins of modern democracy, to the conception shared in this regard by Hobbes, Montesquieu and Bentham.[13] As an example of this view, we may quote the passage cited by Cairns from Bentham: "Property and law are born, and must die together. Before the laws there was no property: take away the laws, all property ceases."[14] Thus property is no longer that substance upon which the law is based but is rather a function of the law. Under this conception contract would no longer remain a mere title of ownership but would become a mandamus to use. The obligation of use would be involved in ownership such that property not used could not remain property. There would be no more privilege to keep others from using but rather the obligation to use for either personal or social purposes.

Realism thus calls for a social theory of property, and

[13] Cf. Cairns, op. cit., p. 71, notes 1–4.
[14] Ibid., p. 72, n. 1.

the outlines of this theory have already been adumbrated by Cairns and others.[15] The social theory of property rests upon the justification of the ownership of property by its social uses. It is thus a functional theory, as opposed to the old ‚ substance theory which has broken down. "The essence of this [functional] theory is that property which involves the discharge of definite personal obligations, which fulfills a social purpose, is morally justifiable and that property which is passive, which is merely a claim on wealth produced by another's labor is morally unjustifiable."[16] More briefly: "The justification of property must depend not upon any *a priori* principle but upon its social effect."[17] The roots of this conception of property go back to Aristotle,[18] and are perhaps best stated by Aquinas,[19] who argued, against Basil and Ambrose, that property in its useful relations was entirely justifiable. Instead of the substance relation, where "A owns B *against* C, where C represents all other individuals,"[20] we have the functional relation, in which A owns B *for* C. Property has relations to its nominal owner beyond those of contractual ownership; both property and owner have common relations to society. The proper use of property would have to mean the adjustment of the property and of its owner to an established criterion of social function. Private property, then, is justified when by being private it furthers the common social good.

[15] *Ibid.*, pp. 74ff. Once again, Cairns' footnote references are of importance.
[16] *Ibid.*, p. 75.
[17] *Ibid.*, p. 78.
[18] *Politics*, ii, 5.
[19] And excellently summarized by Cairns, *op. cit.*, pp. 76–77.
[20] *Ibid.*, p. 59.

The Democratic Function of Property

We have now to ask ourselves, in the light of the foregoing discussion, what would be the effect upon the structure of democracy of the shift from the conception of
property as substance to that of property as function.

As everyone who has considered the question carefully
has readily admitted, democracy grew out of a desire to
protect private property. It was an instrument intended
to establish the rights of the trading class over the classes
of status, the clergy and the nobility. And the rights of
the trading class largely involved property interests. Men
with as widely divergent views as Adam Smith, Bagehot
and Burke, were in agreement with this theory of the purpose of democracy, as Laski has shown.[21] The prophecy
became fulfilled that the "affluence of the rich" would
"excite the indignation of the poor, who are often both
driven by want and prompted by envy to invade their
possessions." [22] The gross inequalities of wealth dictated
that the few would own property beyond their powers of
consumption, while the many would be denied by legal
devices of contract from the satisfaction of impulses toward mere material necessities, such as food and clothing.

Out of the joint enterprise of the trading class, however
small its comparative numbers, and the political protection of private property, however exaggerated its proportions, grew the twin modern giants of democracy and
capitalism. It is essential to recall here that the men who
established the principles of modern democracy were not
all dissemblers. Most of them intended to found govern-

[21] *Parliamentary Government*, pp. 20–22.
[22] *Ibid.*, p. 21, citing Adam Smith.

ment upon a basis of equal right and privilege. They would be nothing short of astounded could they observe today the results of their handiwork: the retention of state power to all intents and purposes in the hands of the comparatively few holders of large properties, the finance capitalists. Whatever the prejudices of Locke and Montesquieu, they did not foresee that power in politics would become almost directly proportional to power in economics allotted by the amount of property owned.

Today we are witnessing the agonies of capitalism in its decline, striving to maintain its position in a period of contracting economy, with the only means at its disposal the mechanism of an economy constructed to operate in an expanding economy. The paramount issue before us is whether capitalism can fall without bringing about the destruction of the democracy with which it has been so closely associated. That arrangement which Professor Laski has so aptly termed "the uneasy marriage between capitalism and democracy" [23] was surely not made in heaven but in eighteenth century Europe; and if this is true then it ought to be possible to bring about an amicable divorce and a satisfactory property settlement. We do not have to save capitalism in order to save democracy, since there is no necessary relation between them.

The principle toward which the foregoing analysis has led is that the key to the peaceful separation of democracy from capitalism, with the consequent preservation of democracy, the best form of government which has yet been discovered, is contained in the change from the theory of property as substance to the theory of property as function. Such a change would require of course a corresponding shift in the individual's view from one of

[23] *Ibid.*, p. 24.

enlightened self-interest to one of enlightened social interest. Has this transition any psychological grounds?
Bishop Butler could have responded to anyone who since
the eighteenth century had sought to alter the drift of
social events, by showing, as he in fact did, that only
some subjective impulses are self-regarding. Other individual impulses, no less owned by the subject, are not
directed toward procuring any change in the individual
himself. Sympathy, for example, is an impulse which has
in many instances proved strong enough even to override
some of the impulses which are self-regarding. What the
individual, so to speak, detaches from society is substantial; what he contributes to that society is functional.
One purpose, at least, of the existence of that substance
is the occurrence of those functions.

In more concrete terms applicable to the present situation, the shift from the understanding of property as
substance to that of property as function would surely
not involve the abolition of private property. For we
have shown that within limits the private ownership of
property is an indispensable arrangement. But it probably would involve the transition from the private to the
public ownership of the means of production, with a view
to securing that production can be continued for use
rather than for profit. Under a democratic government
in which property was expected to serve its proper function, there would be no control exercised by any individual over other individuals, as at present, on the basis of
the superior ownership of substantial properties. The
superiority of individuals would be forced back upon a
more justifiable basis, upon a basis of obligation rather
than of privilege.

Property as substance has in the past admitted an almost unlimited individualism. Socialism tends to stifle such individualism, but democracy need not. There would need to be no end to the extent to which individuals could compete in their rational efforts to excel in their contributions toward the furtherance of the welfare of society. It may be taken as axiomatic that certain individuals are bound to rise superior to others; men are neither born equal nor do they attain to equality. And, furthermore, there is no reason to thrust it on them. The spirit of competition is normal to human individuals. But it is the business of democracy to insure that social conditions of competition and of superiority shall turn the individual's efforts toward the benefit of society as a whole and not allow them to be used against other individuals.

The democratic end can only be accomplished if we raise the level of competitive striving above the economic level of the struggle for subsistence. Men must come to be honored under democratic government not for the amount of property of which they can boast of having deprived society, but rather for how much benefit they have been to society. The honest politician, the scientist, the artist, the inventor, the educator, and the social worker are the logical aristocrats of a democratic society. It is the contention here that this situation can only be brought about through a radical alteration in the theory of property from one of substance to one of function. For such alteration, as we have tried to demonstrate, indicates avenues to the maintenance of democratic government, and the safeguarding of those liberties which it has partly served to bestow.

3.

Orígins

of Democracy in Irrationalism

Irrational Origins of Negative Democracy

THE POLITICAL FORM OF DEMOCRACY, WHICH WE HAD BEEN taught in childhood could be taken for granted as one of the facts of current human experience, is being challenged. It has come as a shock to many that it is possible for democracy to be supplanted, but such is actually the case. Only a short while ago the drift toward the democratic form of government was widespread. Headed by the great democracies of Europe and America, the general tendency was exemplified by the effort of many smaller countries to follow. From the Balkans to South America, new democracies were constituted in the beginning of the present century. But now suddenly the political atmosphere has veered sharply and the tendency has taken a new direction. The intensification of the class struggle has been the occasion for the assaulting of the democratic system upon all sides. Communism and fascism are mortal enemies, yet there is one point upon which they find agreement, and that point is the common dislike and distrust of democracy.

It is in times like these that we find it most advisable to penetrate to fundamental issues. The philosopher flourishes only when implicit assumptions are unearthed and ultimately prior major premises are questioned. New political systems find it necessary to advance behind a barricade of philosophical defenses. Communism has its metaphysics in the writings of Marx and Engels and Lenin, and fascism has its own in the ideologies of Mussolini and of Hitler and Rosenberg. (The term "ideology," by the way, is the new name for the philosophy of politics.) We may well ask how democracy fares in such a competition. Does democracy have its own advocates of a philosophical nature?

Assuredly it does. Democracy being a much older form than either communism or fascism has a longer history of apologetics. Yet curiously, the philosophy of democracy is hardly the imposing subject we should have supposed it would be. No great names stand out; and there are no pretentious systems. There is a reason why the philosophical basis for democracy has never been set forth in any great detail. This failure, however, cannot be legitimately erected into a principle, and there is still another reason why the philosophical basis of democracy must be located and displayed in a position of some importance. In order that the course of our argument for democracy may be clearly understood, it will be necessary to go back to show the origins of modern democracy. Ancient democracy will not be discussed, because the modern form presents peculiarities which are most pertinent to the argument in this place. The elements of democracy, like those of communism and fascism, have been known in other times and under other names; but we shall have to deal here only with recent influences.

How Democracy Came to Be Irrational.—The Englishman, Locke, and the Frenchman, Montesquieu, are cited always as the fathers of modern democracy. These are eighteenth century figures. To a great extent the viewpoint of the eighteenth century was molded by the assumptions of several centuries earlier. Locke and Montesquieu, like all others of their time, came unknowingly under the influence of these assumptions.

The Renaissance was a period of revolt against the dogmatic rationalism of the Middle Ages. To speak of the Middle Ages in this connection is to mean the Church by which it was molded and dominated. Christianity began as a rational movement, but in the course of time its rationalism had hardened, so that what had been argued from rational grounds was later imposed as articles of faith. The result was that rationalism became dogmatic. Now, to speak of dogma and of rationalism in the same breath is a contradiction, but this is not always so evident. The people of the Renaissance thought that they were revolting against reason when they were actually revolting against dogmatism. But since the dogma went about so loudly heralded as reason, the Renaissance people thought they were dissatisfied with reason itself, and hence considered themselves anti-rational. Thus the Renaissance did what all large-scale movements typically do—it went from one extreme to another. From the authority of reason, the new freedom led those who fled to accept unwittingly another authority, that of empiricism. The appeal to brute fact in all matters of doubt was held to be opposed to reason. This was a mistake. Facts act as brakes upon unbridled assumptions; but they do not supplant deductive reasoning. The Renaissance people thought that in beginning their arguments with premises of fact instead of with premises of faith they had obviated the necessity for argument. Nothing could be further from the truth. Consistency, or freedom from contradiction, must govern any successful course of action whether or not we are aware of it.

Be that as it may, however, the main point to be remembered is that the modern age was ushered in under the auspices of irrationalism. A scorn for anything and everything rational has characterized modern activity. The extraordinary advance of mathematics and physical science in the last century and a quarter, both highly rational undertakings, has done nothing to alter this universal prejudice. The mathematicians have generally worked in ignorance of the basis of mathematics, at least until comparatively recent times, and the physical scientists have to their own satisfaction somehow identified reason with philosophy and philosophy with religion. We may say in general that all activities, disciplines and systems having their origins since the seventeenth century have been thought to be in essence irrational.

We are now in a position to see a little of the situation in which Locke and Montesquieu found themselves. The premises to which they knowingly or unknowingly subscribed were twofold. The first premise consisted in the new-found freedom of the individual, liberated from the involuntary imprisonment of a scholastic dogmatism to which reason had but lately failed to give its assent. If there were some indubitable empirical facts which the mediaeval Church philosophy had failed to take into account, why then there must be others; and if there were others, perhaps they were countless; so that mediaeval philosophy, far from continuing to be the most inclusive system, now appeared as a small outworn limitation from which the new scientist was fast breaking away. Thus individual liberty came to be the first premise of all political thinking in the eighteenth century.

Authority, in the eyes of the Renaissance, had earned a bad name. It had come to be identified with coercion. And as we have seen, reason was identified with authority because Church realism had made the claim to rationalism; and hence the new freedom came in the name of irrationalism. The second premise which the political fathers of modern democracy accepted implicitly was the undesirable nature of authority due to its rationalistic coercive nature. It is easy to see that, following upon the two basic principles which Locke and Montesquieu inherited, they must have thought of the whole notion of government as coercive and tyrannical by nature, and restrictive of the liberties of the individual. Their task became one of formulating a political system in which the political rights of the individual would be as great as possible but in which government would be as little of an interfering sort as it could conveniently be made. The best government was thought to be the least government.

Some Shortcomings of Negative Democracy.—The result was that democracy came to be identified, more or less officially, with a minimum of sovereignty and with the maximum adoption of the theory of the separation of powers. The decline of sovereignty was marked by the severe limiting of governmental authority, by the acquiescence of the state in the right of citizens to sue it in certain cases, and finally by the delegation of much of central governmental powers to the lesser authority of individual states. These moves, based on the distrust of central authority, were intended to weaken it in such a manner that its authority could not become focused upon any one individual. The modern democrat resents any display of political authority from the home office. More typical still is the deep resentment of the average Frenchman, peasant as well as middle class, to the taxing power. Corruption having had so long a political history, he tends to think of taxation either as confiscation or as robbery, aimed only at the betterment of those in authority.

That the democratic devices did weaken the central authority of the government cannot very well be disputed. Indeed, so incapacitated is government rendered by democracy that war is only made possible by the temporary extension of extraordinary powers. In the last World War, the systems of democracy met this challenge well; they functioned by means of extraordinary powers, and as soon as the War was over, they relinquished these powers and dropped back into the old position of acting merely as a necessary evil, confining their extra attention to the debt problem, the returning soldiers, and other problems of rehabilitation. Wars cannot be fought along democratic lines because fighting requires rigid organization emanating from the highest political authorities. Hence democracy is essentially an anti-war system of government. Considering the fact that governments of all sorts have so long a history of war-waging, this fact is strongly in democracy's favor. In a world in which the chief function of government has always been the defense of its own borders or the invasion of others, to discover a system of government which is inherently opposed to armed conflict, and to put it into effect even for a little while is assuredly a gain for civilization.

However, the opposition to war is not the whole story. A government so weak that it is able successfully to resist the temptation to use force might very well fall an easy prey to organized efforts from within which are aimed at its eventual destruction. The presence of war is an attack aimed at government from without. But there are other attacks aimed from within, and these latter democracy is ill equipped to fight. One attack from within may be given the name of economic monopoly. Democracy is exclusively a political system. Failing to recognize the close relation between politics and economics, political democracy took no safeguards against the economic peril of autocracy while there was time. The result is that economic autocracy endangers political democracy from within.

Political democracy provided for the franchise. It was anxious that as many persons as possible should have a voice in the making of political decisions both great and small. But it did not have a word to say about economic salvation or destruction, except to remark that this must be at the discretion of the individual. It can be said in the defense of the origins of modern democracy that it was thought that all able-bodied persons willing to work for their own economic welfare would have no difficulty in finding—or making—the opportunity to do so. It assumed that those persons poorly equipped would get along, and that the best equipped would prosper, each according to his just deserts. It said, however, very little upon the subject, deeming economic questions to be natural ones and all social regulation an infringement of liberties.

As we now know, the best equipped did prosper. In many cases they prospered at the expense of others. The coming of technological industrialism, the power tool, and vast population increases, conspired to provide a situation which none of the democratic fathers had ever anticipated. A few persons managed to gain control of the majority of available wealth, while for most persons even a minimal survival became a matter of terrific anxiety, privation, and narrow margins. And many millions more found any economic existence all but impossible and came to live at the starvation level or unsatisfactorily upon the bounty of the government.

The spectacle of starvation in the midst of plenty makes the democratic situation an intolerable one from the political point of view. But when we turn to look at what has happened to the political system itself under the stress and strain of actual application, we do not find any excellence with which to console ourselves. We see only that the economic disparity which political democracy has allowed to develop is penetrating to such a point into the political life that it endangers the very continuance of political democracy. Those suffering economic privation threaten to organize in the effort to gain greater political influence. Those in control of the lion's share use every ounce of their political influence to keep economic affairs in *status quo*. Their efforts in this direction tend to become unscrupulous in the extreme, and so the whole economic struggle has more than a fair chance of disrupting political democracy.

The failure of political democracy to cope with economic inequalities lets the barriers down so that other weaknesses which were never before apparent now come clearly into view. Modern events challenge the democratic form in a way which reveals fundamental shortcomings of a highly serious nature. The inability to act swiftly, the failure to make and to keep positive decisions, and complete bewilderment when faced with the urgent necessity of dealing effectively with governments of a different political persuasion, show up as monstrous weaknesses. Recent occurrences have demonstrated that democracies are slow at a time when speedy action may be necessary to meet a challenge; they are vacillating and indecisive in situations demanding a firm stand; and they have a tendency to yield on any show of force by other governments which do not suffer the same difficulties.

Requirements for a Positive Democracy

The question which it is imperative that we ask ourselves is: Are these difficulties inherent in the very nature of systematic democracy, or are they merely evidence of the misapplication to government of true democratic principles?

It is becoming increasingly evident that most people, including even those who live as citizens in the democracies, no longer believe as they once did in the superior virtues of the democratic form of government. Despite the fact that nothing is ever gained by the appeal to force in the form of violence, it remains true that when you no longer believe in what you have, sufficiently to make you ever ready and willing to fight for it, then you have nothing to defend. Since no political system has ever been either ideal or ideally applied, we cannot offer a decisive answer one way or the other to the question which we have set ourselves. The difficulties, however, seem to be rather with applications than with principles. It is the thesis of this chapter that the reason democratic peoples no longer have a profound belief in democracy is not because the democratic principles are unsound but rather because they are misinterpreted—largely due to the peculiar way in which their application was started and has been continued.

If it is true that democracy as a political system of government is, relatively speaking, self-consistent, and that the present difficulties of the democracies are due in large part to the way in which democracy has been applied, then it behooves us to approach the problem from that point of view and to discover what is wrong with its application. Obviously, the business of application has its roots in the peculiar emphasis given to democracy by the revolt against the systems of government which it came to supplant.

Let us re-examine the philosophical basis of democracy, this time with a critical eye. The dialectical method of establishing social movements is always partially suspect. That the evils of bad government can be eliminated by substituting for one government proved bad, another of the opposite type, is a species of argument which contains an undistributed middle. Opposites do not exhaust possible alternatives, and it is always likely that the old system which was abandoned bag and baggage contained some merit, just as it is equally likely that the new system, which is adopted enthusiastically on the premise that nothing else could be more different from the old, will contain many disadvantages. The choosing of antitheses is an unlucky way of looking for satisfactory solutions, as even the dialecticians themselves admit when they set up the further goal of synthesis.

We have characterized the old form of democracy as we have come to know it on the basis of its philosophical postulates, as negative democracy. By negative democracy is meant the effort to make democracy supply the function of government under a philosophy which denies the essential necessity for real government. Irrationalism which put the whole of human reality in the individual and which allowed none to society called for a form of government which was to be considered as a necessary evil and thus held to a minimum. Democracy as the attempt to supply a government under a philosophy which deemed no real government necessary was sure to be a negative affair. But there is another form of democracy possible, and this other form, based on different philosophical postulates, we may term positive democracy. Positive democracy would have to include among other things the following: a rational philosophy; a positive theory of the function of government; economic regulations; and a theory of rights. We may consider each of these separately.

A Positive Rational Philosophy.—A rational philosophy would have to base itself upon a realistic metaphysics and not upon the nominalistic metaphysics which was the support of the older negative democracy. Society is composed of the relations between individuals. According to realism, social organization is as real as (although no more real than) [1] the individual. Indeed each item to be considered can be analyzed into the elements of an organization. Just as social organization consists of human individuals taken as elements of analysis, so the human individual consists of organs, cells, and electrons

[1] Hegel considered the state to be more real than the individual because it is more valuable. The error is due to a mistaken identification of reality with value. The state may (or may not) be more valuable than any given individual. But this in any case would not make it more real. Reality is not a meaningful term except in contrast with illusion. The use of "reality" with "value," "appearance" or any other notion, is an error. Minimal values are real values just as appearances are real appearances.

taken as lower elements of analysis. The fact that social organizations are interchangeable and individual organizations are not does not argue for the illusory or mental status of social organizations. Social organizations differ with regard to their value, and it is the task of social science to discover their relative merits so that there will be defensible grounds for preferring one social organization to another.

The old canon of nominalism was, as we have seen, William of Occam's "Razor," which pronounced that entities must not be multiplied beyond necessity. By this he meant that we cannot justifiably increase the number of names to account for things to a greater number than the things themselves required. The difficulty here lies with the enumeration of things. Are physical things the only things? In that case society does not matter and the individual does. The individual has physical being; but the search for a physical social organization leaves us with the counting of heads and the sad conclusion that society is nothing more than the addition-group of real human individuals. However, the error of nominalism lies in supposing that the only real things are physical things.

We can confute the argument almost on its own grounds. For if we carry it one step further and include with physical things their motion (which incidentally the materialists from Democritus to Marx have always done), then we must arrive at the proposition that a thing is known by its effects. And on this ground, we cannot escape the conclusion that social organization must be as real as the individual. Assuredly, social organizations have worked more physical effects, for good or ill, than individuals by themselves ever have or could.

And if social organizations are things having physical effects, then there must be names for them as well as for individuals and this, too, on an equal basis. The principle of "Occam's Razor" has always been stated negatively: "entities must *not* be multiplied *beyond* necessity." The other side of the question also demands expression: entities *must* be multiplied *to* necessity. Thus social organizations are things just as much as are human individuals.

We shall learn in the next subdivision just what conclusions with regard to government are implied by the necessary changes from nominalism to realism and from social organization as addition-group to social organization as thing. Meanwhile, it must be pointed out that there are important conclusions bearing on the general theory of politics which should result. These are the questions of (1) sovereignty and (2) the separation of powers.

(1) Sovereignty has been held in the past to be possessed by one of the following: a God, a Church, a state, an individual, a group of individuals, a class, a race, a specific doctrine, or a combination of any of these. For instance, during the Middle Ages sovereignty was divided between Church and state; in modern Germany, sovereignty is divided between an individual (Hitler) and a race (the so-called Nordic). In the United States of America, sovereignty is held to reside in the people as a whole by virtue of a specific doctrine (the Constitution). None of these, not even the last, is conformable with a rational philosophy of government. For a rational philosophy maintains that no authority can be considered superior to the dictates of reason. Logic, a rational philosophy must insist, is the final authority, and by logic here is meant the law of non-contradiction. Scientific

method, as we shall see in a later chapter,[2] is an extension to the principle of actual discovery of that logical law. Thus the sovereignty of reason is incompatible with any dogmatically established sovereign authority.

The authorities which war for sovereignty in political organizations are not, however, on a par with regard to their amenableness to reason. God, for instance, is a meaningless notion when considered as an absolute one. None of us has any way of knowing what is God's will with respect to the political field as a whole. Since by definition the notion of God embraces everything, to make an appeal to Him is not to make any finite distinction. Yet finite distinctions of validity and value in the jungle of political theory are just what is needed and what, in fact, a theory of sovereignty attempts to supply. In its degenerate form, the appeal to God for sovereignty becomes the appeal to His Representative: the will of a Churchman, such as the Pope. In this case the surrender to an individual's will is irrational, and this is equally true whether the individual be a Churchman, a political dictator, or any other.

A doctrine, such as that contained in the Constitution of the United States, is far more rational than any of the other proffered alternatives competing for the label of sovereign. Even here, however, the exception must be made that the doctrine itself should be alterable in the light of any irrational elements whenever such elements are brought into view. The Constitution, happily, contains provision for such an eventuality. In the last analysis, sovereignty must reside in the principles of reason, "to the end it may be a government of laws and not of men." [3]

---

[2] Chapter VII.

[3] The Massachusetts Declaration of Rights, 1.xxx, adopted in 1780.

Rationality is not self-founded. Beneath rationality lies faith in reason. Reason and its laws are not human inventions but only human discoveries. *Faith* in reason is, like all other faiths, irrational. Its defense is that, unlike all other faiths, it can be defended by reason, and we are, among other things, reasoning beings. Thus the Constitution of a democracy as well as any laws founded upon it, must be held to be the best representative of what men have found reason to demand in the political field. But the discovery of the demands of reason in the political field is a human affair and thus fallible; whatever doctrines are adopted must stand ready for such alteration as later processes of reasoning might demonstrate to be necessary.

(2) To the end that democratic government might be of laws and not of men, the democracies have undertaken certain safeguards whose task it is to prevent the usurpation of governmental powers by particular men. The theory of the separation of powers is at least as ancient as Aristotle.[4] His division was the threefold one of the public assembly, the officers of the state, and the judiciary. For Locke, these became the legislative, executive and federative.[5] The final treatment was given by Montesquieu, who divided the powers into the legislative, the executive and the judicial,[6] which is the form which they have in the American democracy of today. As Cairns points out, one attack upon the theory of the separation of powers has come from legal theory with the charge that the separation cannot be rendered absolute and in

[4] *Politics*, i, 1, and iv, 14–16. For this reference as well as for much of the data of this section, I am indebted to the excellent chapter on Political Theory in Huntington Cairns' *Law and the Social Sciences*.
[5] *Two Treatises of Civil Government*, Bk. II, Chap. XII.
[6] *Spirit of Laws*, Bk. VI, Chap. VI.

certain applications is extremely vague. The courts have fought shy, whenever they conveniently could, of defining the specific duties of office under the triad of categories. But the question at issue here is not one of the abstract justification of the theory of the separation of powers but rather of the method of its proper application. The bad application of a theory to practice is not by itself sufficient to disprove the theory.

Another attack upon the theory of the separation of powers has come from those who charge that the separation of powers tends to be disorganizing. Hegel, among others, was concerned over this question, and tried to bring the separated powers together again in a dialectical unity. Of course, he was correct in that it is essential that the separated powers form a unity, although not in the elevated and severe sense encompassed by Hegel in his conception of the state as "the Divine Idea as it exists on earth." [7] This is the language of dogmatic rationalization, not of rational scientific experimentation. Reason requires that the three powers function harmoniously and interdependently. The unity which Hegel should have sought is that to which Edward Livingston, the classical Louisiana jurist, once called attention: the unity of the separation of powers in their practical application, the "unity of textual formulation and judicial practice," [8] for example.

Positive democracy must be concerned to preserve for the individual all those liberties to which as an individual he is entitled. The separation of powers is one device which has been constructed to forestall tyranny. It is

[7] Hegel, *Philosophy of Right*, Sec. 272.
[8] Mitchell Franklin, "Hegel on the American Constitutional Crisis," read before the International Congress of Comparative Law, The Hague, August 5, 1937.

not without its shortcomings and limitations, but any alternative theory which wishes to supplant it while maintaining the same definitely democratic end in view will have to show a superior justification by reason. The popular assembly, impossible in our present vast populations, has been replaced by the assembly of duly-elected representatives of the people. It is their task to make the laws in the light of what reason allows, given the raw material of actual conditions. The executive with his police power has to see to their execution. And the judiciary has to adjudicate conflicts of a social nature in the light of the established laws. Within a given range of fallibility the system is a rational one.

A Positive Theory of the Function of Government.— Positive democracy must include a positive theory of the function of government. As T. H. Green has pointed out, society may at times be a "hindrance of hindrances," but it also has a positive rôle to play in the individual's attainment of the good life.[9] Green, it is true, defines the function of government as the allowance of a full development to the individual, which is a definition of the purpose of the whole in terms of its parts. Now, since the purpose of a whole must lie partly outside itself, society has in all probability a function beyond as well as within social organization. Yet the narrow definition of the function of society as the service of the individuals which go to compose it is true also, but only within limits. Green's contribution consists in his premise that there must be a set of natural social laws to which man-made social laws approximate, and that there must be possible an ideal society whose laws would be identical

---

[9] For an outline of T. H. Green's realistic views of the function of government, see Joad, *op. cit.*, pp. 551 ff.

with natural law. The government of society, then, is in itself a good.

We have seen that democracy conceived on a negative basis holds the function of government to be that of a necessary evil. But, as we have also seen, this is a misconception, tenable only if the function of government be held to be that of a coercive power. Government is never coercive except in cases where its authority is challenged from within or without; negative government may be coercive, but positive government is regulative. Its task is to legislate, to execute and to adjudicate all activities falling within the field of the social aspect of the individual. Even without a conflict of interests, these require regulation. Let us give some examples. The adjustments of boundary lines between properties held by individuals, where confusion is detrimental to the interests of both parties; the preservation of natural resources, including precautions against forest fires; the care of natural waterways; national defense, public instruction, civil legislation, foreign affairs—these are only a few of the functions of government which give evidence of its non-coercive nature. Coercion is a product either of the non-acceptance of the principles of government or of the corruption of men in office. The true nature of government is regulative.

Positive Economic Regulations.—All governments are required to provide for the welfare of their citizens. Democracy is untenable except on a system of liberties; and these the fathers of democracy tried very hard to establish. Political liberties along classical lines were expressly provided for in the writing of the Constitution. We cannot blame the makers of the Constitution for their failure to foresee difficulties which might arise but of which there was no hint in their day. These new difficulties have proved to be of an economic nature.[10] In a later chapter [11] it will be shown just what happens when an economic inequality threatens to overthrow a political democracy by upsetting the balance of power. The new economic difficulty consists in the retention of inordinate social power by a few individuals by means of industrialism, the system of mass production employing the power tool. Ownership of the means of production allows for the informal wielding of political power, and thus for the destruction of that political balance of power whose strength lies in the vote of a majority subscribing to the rule of reason and calling for legislation in the best interests of the total population.

The social concern of government with society as a whole "places upon it the necessity of safeguarding the interests of all of its members from the 'blind' effects of the activities of some of them." [12] This is seen to be especially true in the case of the economic sphere of interests. Economic conditions are the result of economic relations between individuals but have social consequences beyond individual control. Economics thus becomes very much the business of government. "Equality" and the "pursuit of happiness" are not expressions meaning that men are born equal and have an equal

---

[10] The American Bill of Rights confined itself to political rights. The inclusion of economic rights was not, however, entirely outside the boundaries of custom in these matters. Article 21 of the Jacobin Constitution of 1793 states: "Les secours sont une dette sacrée. La société doit la subsistance aux citoyens malheureux, soit en leur procurant du travail, soit en assurant les moyens d'exister à ceux qui sont hors d'état de travailler." Larousse, Grand dictionnaire universal, IV, 1041.
[11] Chapter X.
[12] Joad, op. cit., p. 777.

right to do nothing. What is meant is rather that men are born equal with regard to their *opportunities* and should have an equal right of access to those material and cultural possessions of society which are necessary for the full development of the potentialities of the individual.[13]

Any democracy wishing to survive must provide for economic regulations such that the proper disposal of the profits of production and distribution will never bring about the unbalanced possession of power. Self-correction of economic excesses by economic sanctions is an extremely delicate undertaking, and one likely to engender the overthrow of everything for which democracy stands. The Marxists are correct in their charge that vested interests will abandon all principles in their efforts to defend acquired properties. But although this renders the task very difficult, it is not an impossible one. The adoption of a certain number of socialist measures does not have to mean the advent of communism any more than it means the abandonment of democracy. Monopoly capitalism is capable of rendering democracy a matter of mere lip-service and not an effective form of government. Change, therefore, may be change in the direction of democracy as well as away from it. One Constitutional amendment would be capable of correcting the oversight of the original makers of American liberty.

A *Positive Theory of Rights.*—The theory of rights is the final point on which a positive democracy will have to assert its nature. Since the question of civil rights is analyzed somewhat more fully in Chapter IX, it will be unnecessary to argue the question here. Suffice it to

[13] *Ibid.*, pp. 801–02.

state for the present that the traditional civil rights are not on a parity, and moreover suffer from an exclusion. The right to the freedom of opinion is one of which, even under an absolutistic dictatorship, we cannot as yet be robbed. No one knows what we are thinking, and until some means is devised of finding out we are free to think what we like, whether it suits the government or not. Freedom of expression and of assembly is another question. Freedom of expression should go unqualified, but freedom of assembly should not, having in mind that ever-present weakness of the tendency of democracy toward mob rule. The wording of the Constitution is quite correct: "peaceably to assemble." Every day it has been possible to stand on the corner of an English square, listening to an orator haranguing the crowd, while a policeman hovers watchfully by but remains passive. Anything may be said so long as it cannot be interpreted as incitement to violence. A people which is not free to express its opinion in print or by voice is not a democratic people.

The omission referred to in the list of civil rights is the right to work. The right of individuals to work was never a compelling one in the kind of agricultural democracy which the United States represented in its beginnings. But an economic democracy engenders new conditions which make this right imperative, and to some extent dependent upon governmental function. Positive democracy cannot permit an exclusive usurpation of economic prerogatives by individual citizens such that any large minority is deprived of the right. Deprivation of this kind is detrimental to all citizens, including those supposedly benefiting by the economic monopoly, whether or not the latter are aware of it. Political democracy is responsible for the welfare of the totality of citizens, and hence for any economic system which may be adopted. Democratic government must be held accountable for democratic principles even when these come into conflict with economic situations. Thus industrial democracy would seem to be the only system compatible with a positive interpretation of democracy.

We have come a long way from our inquiry into the origins of democracy in irrationalism. We have noted that although democracy was inclined by its origins toward an irrationalism, it is better supported on a rational basis than on an irrational one. Democracy today is assailed upon all sides, and gives promise of being abandoned altogether as unworkable. But it is fair to assert that democracy has not failed; rather the failure is of a rational democracy with irrational foundations. Given the proper philosophical justification it may survive. What we see challenged today is not democracy but the false foundations to which it clings mistakenly owing to an accident of origins. Democracy is the rule of reason, and the rule of reason is rooted in the welfare of the many and in their conviction of its justification. Democracy perishes before coercion from within because force in this sense is not rational. Democracy must rest upon the persuasion of its philosophical rationality, and not upon internal coercion or force in any form. Democracy must not be abandoned because of the inability to defend it rationally; in the rational sense it has never been tried. Let us only assume that democracy, regardless of what its origins have been or what its corruptions may be, is a possible form of rational government, and we shall be on our way toward the democratic experiment of government by reason.

PART II

THEORETICAL ASPECTS

4.

Political Fashions in Epistemology

In the following chapters of part ii, the plan is to show some of the implications of democratic theory. We may be able to gain a broader perspective upon our topic if we depart from its narrow analysis for a moment and consider a few far-reaching implications. First, the relation between epistemology, the theory of knowledge, and democracy will be studied; and in order to see this relationship in its proper light other contemporary political doctrines will have to be examined in the same connection. In Chapter V, we shall seek out the relation between democracy and the current development of ontology, or the theory of being. A new tendency in philosophy will be revealed in its alliance with the positive interpretation of democracy. Anthropology will be asked, in Chapter VI, to contribute toward a better general understanding of individualism, which has played so large a part in democracy. In Chapter VII, we shall turn our attention to science, and, after setting forth a brief abstract analysis of scientific method, enter into the question of whether democracy as one branch of rational empirical practice can be identified with any effort to apply scientific method in the political field. Chapter VIII will adduce the widest considerations of ethics as these are conformable with the kind of principles we should like to see at work in democracy. Finally, Chapter IX will consist of an analysis of those principles of liberalism which are built into the foundations of democracy, without which no democracy can be, and with which other systems can be said to be closely allied with democracy by virtue of containing important democratic elements.

Let us return first, then, to the question of the problem of knowledge, in its relation to democracy. Before arriving at any political conclusions from the problem of knowledge, it will be necessary to examine *in abstracto* the chief theories regarding knowledge and to consider their relative merits.

The Three Basic Theories of Knowledge

There are three basic positions, and only three, which can be taken up with regard to the process of knowledge. All possible epistemologies are variations of some sort on one of them. The three positions are located as a result of attempts to answer the question of how that which is known can enter into the knowledge relation. We shall see what these epistemologies are, endeavor to order them according to their degree of correctness, and show which of them is assumed behind the current political philosophies.

The vast majority of philosophers agree that in the process of knowing there is a subject who knows, an object which is known, and a relation between them. Another way of presenting this fact is to say that there is only one function, namely that of knowing, a relation having subjective and objective end-terms. Now, epistemologies vary according as they choose one or another of these end-terms, or the relation itself, and declare it the most important. The problem may always be formulated as the determination of what contributes to the knowledge process that which is known. Now there are only five alternative ways of solving this problem. These are to assume that what is known (1) is contributed by the subject (mentalism); (2) comes through the subject, e.g., from the mind of God (idealism); (3) arises from the relation between subject and object (modified subjectivism or relativism); (4) is contributed by the object (materialism); (5) comes through the object, e.g., from possibility (realism). Let us consider each of these separately.

The first answer to the problem, then, is to assume that the subject of knowledge, the observer, contributes the content of knowledge to the knowledge process. Among the adherents of this solution are found the various and often warring types of subjective philosophies: idealism, pragmatism, radical empiricism, some forms of voluntarism, and finally solipsism. Each of these separate philosophies can, however, eventually be driven back to the solipsistic position which asserts that the subject of knowledge is the sole creator of that which is known. For in each case the existence of the objective world is held negligible as something unknowable in its reality, and the criterion of knowledge confined to the experiencing subject. Solipsism simply goes the whole way with this position and frankly maintains that the objective world not only does not count but is nonexistent. Thus the subject becomes the creator of his entire world, both animate and inanimate, in all its remotest ramifications, and with all its contradictions and disvalues. Percepts and concepts (which are values and relations considered in their mental apprehension) take the place of material bodies.

This extremist position is one which has from time to time been held explicitly, but which it is hard to suppose anyone profoundly believes. If my neighbor insists on maintaining that he has created his own world together with everything in it, including me, his Ford, and the star Aldebaran, there is no way in which I can prove him in error, although I must rest convinced that even he does not believe in such a silly theory. Unless the burden of the proof is put upon him to explain how he created such a world, or, if it is a dream, why he does not awaken, the theory is logically irrefutable. But it is also finally undemonstrable and therefore unacceptable.

The second alternative need not detain us for very long. The hypothesis which asserts that the subject contributes what is known to the knowledge process but receives it in turn from the mind of God, is open to all the criticisms which have already been leveled against the first alternative. This is the position of Berkeley and is termed subjective idealism. Whether or not solipsism is avoided by throwing the responsibility for the creative act of the cognitional process back upon God is highly debatable. Certainly it is a truth of logic that all appeals to the identity of a first principle lying beyond the actual world, in explanation of the differentiae of this actual world, are illicit. However much devotion may be laid at the feet of a final cause, this still will not account for the distinctions between efficients. Since God, in the case of subjective idealism, admittedly works through human minds, the problem is put forward again to the necessity of determining how human minds create the content of their own knowledge. At this point, we are faced with all the difficulties which lie in the path of the acceptance of mentalism.

The majority of the subjectivist epistemologies attempt to effect a compromise, and this leads us to a consideration of our third alternative. Those who today deal with epistemology to the exclusion of ontology, believing that the latter has been assigned to physics and that only by such a retreat can the philosophers themselves become hard-headed, experimental, and safely scientific, are led into the compromise theory. For epistemology isolated from ontological considerations is likely to lead nowhere. Preoccupation with epistemology always tacitly presupposes the effort to discover the grounds for an ontology, anyway.

The present tendency is to make mixtures of subjective and objective contributions in various proportions, in the hope that whatever the elements are in the concoction they will fuse into a blend. The assumption here is that the object of knowledge is what is known, but that the extent of its objective independence is indeterminable, owing to the fact that the subject's own perception colors all knowledge of the object. This interference by the subject's own intrusion into the knowing process confuses the issue past where the various elements, which are supposed to be contributed by the subject and object respectively, can any longer be separated out and exactly determined. In the group which offers this solution to the epistemological problem belong all those fashionable philosophers whose caution forbids them from making any plunge into ontology. This alternative may be termed Kantian, since it is close to the epistemology of Kant and his successors.

Unfortunately for the effort at compromise, these half-way affairs usually prove to be failures because they succeed in solving nothing. All forms of modified subjectivism in the theory of knowledge fall back into the subjective group. For in any such mixture it is usually admitted that what the subject contributes to knowledge colors what the object contributes, to such an extent that the object itself is rendered indeterminable. Hence the object, hidden behind a permanent veil, becomes relatively unimportant. In fact, it is regarded as so slightly existent that the whole theory is forced to hang upon the subjective contribution. The composite theory of modified subjectivism wants to be objective but is led astray by the fact that objects vary for different subjects and for the same subject upon different occasions. This fact eventually leads explanation completely away from the consideration that an independent object of knowledge may exist. Together with the confused recognition that the subject is not alone in contributing to knowledge, goes a refusal to dismiss the subject's contribution altogether.

The next theory we have to consider is the objective theory of materialism. Materialism supposes that the subject of knowledge merely *knows*, and contributes to the process nothing of what is known. It assigns the con-*tent* of knowledge directly to the object and further supposes that all knowledge is a product of the object impinging in some manner on the subject. Thus the object of knowledge itself owns the knowledge which it produces for the subject.

This is the materialistic theory of knowledge. It is the epistemology of all forms of materialism, of mechanistic materialism as well as of the more prominent dialectical materialism. Its final invalidity can be demonstrated in a number of ways. First, it can be refuted on the basis that it calls for the ownership of attributes by objects, which is not allowable. Objects do not own qualities as permanent attributes. For instance, the glowing tip of a cigarette appears scarlet in sunlight but gold under electric light. What color is it "really"? Again, there is the straight stick which appears bent when half-submerged in water, the penny which appears elliptical and then round, and so on. At least, if objects do own qualities and other properties, we must admit that it is difficult and indeed quite impossible to determine which they own.

The second refutation of the materialistic theory of the knowledge process may be taken from the subatomic studies of modern physics. Materialism presupposes the final reality of material objects of knowledge. But physical analysis has always striven to reduce material particles as far as possible, in order to determine just what the final real particles of matter are. The theories of philosophical atomism, from Democritus to Newton, have acted as safeguards for the prevention of any infinite reduction of matter past materiality by setting up real particles (atoms) as ultimate. Yet modern physics has gone past atoms through various substages of electronic particles to the emission of radiant energy in erg-seconds. Now if the real constituent of matter proves to be quanta of energy, it cannot still be irreducible material particles. Thus materialism stands disproved, and the theory of the ownership of qualities and other attributes is rendered untenable.

What does this refutation of the materialistic theory of knowledge accomplish? Does it drive epistemology to return to some compromise form of the subjective theory? Not at all; for there is yet another alternative to be considered. The fifth alternative is closer to materialism than it is to any of the subjective theories, yet differs from it sufficiently to save it from the usual dangers. This last theory states that the content of knowledge in the knowledge process is not contributed by the subject and not owned by the object. It asserts that what is known enters the process of knowledge *through* the object of knowledge.

The understanding of this theory may be aided by illustration. Let us suppose that we have a blue book. That we do see blue is indubitable, but we do not contribute the blueness to the book by the mere fact of our apprehension of it. Nor is the blueness owned by the book, since its color will change perceptibly under colored lights. The fact is that the blueness is contributed to our knowledge by the book, that is to say blueness enters the knowledge process through the book. It is true that if we did not enter into the act of perceiving books or other blue-colored objects, we would not see the color of blue, but that is a question of our own participation in a perspective. For colors are not owned by objects; they simply enter the knowledge process through them.

This fifth alternative to the solution of the knowledge problem is known as the realistic theory. It is held in various ways and to various degrees by those philosophers who term themselves realists. In the realistic alternative, the question of knowledge is closely associated with that of ontology. With some realists, epistemology is not the all-important problem of philosophy at all, but merely a preliminary inquiry, opening the gateway to more significant problems of ontology. Thus the question is asked immediately, where do the attributes of objects arise? If qualities and other properties are not owned by objects but merely come through them into the act of knowing, where do they come *from?* This question is important, for it is posed in terms of knowledge theory but involves an answer in terms of ontology.

We saw that with subjective idealism the mind of God had to be posited as the origin of all knowledge entering into the process of knowledge through the subject. But with knowledge entering into the process of knowledge through the object, no real entity and no location in time or space has to be posited as origin. What is assumed is merely that there are two equally real orders of being: actuality, characterized by partiality and change; and possibility, characterized by completeness and permanence. Actuality is that world in which we live and have our adventures; it is the world in which the knowledge process occurs. Possibility means merely possibility *of actualization.* It is not a place nor a collection of things. It is merely the undifferentiated conditional prospect of happenings in the future. Possibility is the origin of the content of knowledge which enters into the process through the object.

One of the tests of the validity of a theory is the determination of the extent of its explanatory value. Let us then ask the realistic theory of knowledge to explain the problem of the glowing cigarette end, which appears scarlet in sunlight and gold under electric light. It is at once obvious that the cigarette is not expected to "own" either of these colors; nor does the subject's own perception originate them. The cigarette contributes them to the perceptual process in each case, but the determination for the appearance of color as scarlet or gold hinges upon what we may call the perspective involved. A perspective is a point of view from which an observer takes his readings and in which an object is read. Thus what is scarlet from one perspective is gold from another. The perspective point of view in this case is not peculiar to any subject but may be assumed by any observer; thus it is in no sense subjective, but rather objective, and, further, itself independent of the object.

The realistic epistemology seems able to answer the objection which modern subatomic physics offers to the materialistic epistemology. If all natural objects are reducible to energy relations, then some of these relations are what reach the subject through the object of knowledge. The object is no longer expected to own attributes, but is still expected (as with materialism) to contribute them to the knowledge relation. The material world, according to modern physics, is resolvable into determinate relations having spatio-temporal references, and these determinate relations, according to realistic epistemology, are knowable by the subject through a perspective on the material object of knowledge. Thus once again, the realistic epistemology seems to offer a better explanation than the other proffered alternatives.

Political Choices in Knowledge Theory

Having surveyed the possible alternatives in the field of epistemology, we may now turn to the chief aim of this chapter, which is to identify the three opposed political epistemologies of fascism, communism and democracy with those we have discussed, and to evaluate their truth-content accordingly.

It is very evident that fascism or naziism, as exemplified in Germany, accepts the first of our epistemological alternatives. The philosophy of fascism calls for a mentalistic theory of knowledge. Numerous nazi apologists have called upon their nationals to "think with their blood," to return to "real" life as opposed to the intellectual life. Hitler himself in *Mein Kampf* has advised his countrymen "not to seek out objective truth in so far as it may be favorable to others, but uninterruptedly to serve one's own truth." These quotations, out of many that could be culled, are sufficient to indicate that fascism has accepted not only a mentalism but a mentalism with all its terrifically logical consequences. The nazi doctrine does indeed accept the reduction to which, as we have indicated, mentalism must lead: solipsism, or what Santayana terms a "solipsism of the present moment."

Communism, on the other hand, accepts the philosophy of dialectical materialism. And dialectical materialism is committed to the fourth alternative which we have already set forth: namely, that objects of knowledge themselves contribute the content of knowledge to the knowledge process. Obviously, neither fascism nor communism accepts the fifth alternative of the realistic epistemology, which is here asserted to be the correct one. But it remains to evaluate the two political epistemologies in terms of the one we have chosen as the more correct.

Although neither of the two theories is completely true, it is still important to estimate what truth there is in each. He who thinks that ninety is a hundred is not as wrong as he who thinks that five is a hundred, although ideally speaking both are wrong, as Aristotle well said.

From what has already been set forth in estimation of the various epistemological theories, it should be evident that the materialistic epistemology is far more correct, and contains far more truth, than the mentalistic epistemology. To believe that the subject of knowledge contributes what is known to the act of knowing, as the mentalistic fascists do believe, is to be as much in error concerning the knowledge process as it is possible to be. On the other hand, to believe that the object of knowledge contributes what is known to the act of knowing is almost correct, in the light of our chosen criterion. For it is not a far step from asserting that the object of knowledge contributes the content of knowledge, to asserting that the object of knowledge contributes but does not itself own the content of knowledge.

No democratic political system has explicitly avowed any preference in epistemology. Therefore the argument here will be rather to show that the realistic epistemology is logically more compatible with democracy than are the other alternatives. By realistic epistemology is meant our fifth choice: that knowledge reaches the subject *through* the object of knowledge from possibility, but is not owned by either end-term of the process. Despite its highly individualistic origins in eighteenth century rationalism, democracy was not successfully committed by Montesquieu and Locke to the denial of social law based on reason. Democracy wishes to hold law down to a minimum of what is required, but this is a precaution against dogmatism and does not itself constitute an acceptance of irrationalism. Hence the radically individual epistemology of mentalism and relativism is rejected. And since materialistic epistemology involves a brand of dogmatic absolutism with regard to what exists here and now, it must be likewise rejected by democracy. All that remains, then, is the legalistic theory of realistic epistemology.

Realism holds that all political hypotheses with regard to what things actually are must be susceptible of continual modification in terms of what it is discovered things ought to be. Of course as actuality changes, our knowledge of what ought to be changes with it. All modifications are obliged to follow an increasing knowledge of the truth gained through acquaintance with social legality by means of those glimpses into the nature of things which are caught with the aid of experience. We seek always final law; what we get is efficient law, and we get it by means of hypotheses built upon knowledge which enters through the object of knowledge, theories built upon facts conveying but not owning them.

We may conclude, then, from the findings of our short survey that the fascist epistemology is almost entirely in error, that the communist epistemology is almost correct, and that the democratic philosophy is most clearly open to reconciliation with the realistic epistemology.

Although neither explicit theory of knowledge as politically held is absolutely true, the communist theory of knowledge contains far more truth than does the fascist theory. "To be a materialist," said Lenin in his *Materialism and Empirio-Criticism*, "is to acknowledge objective truth revealed by our sense organs." [1]   But, as Engels admitted, there does exist an absolute truth. The epistemological process in our actual world is the dialectical approach of knowledge toward this absolute truth. It only remains to demonstrate to the communist phi-

[1] (New York, 1927), p. 104.

losophers that the realistic epistemology does not involve, but on the contrary specifically denies, any and every kind of idealism and mentalism. And when this has been accomplished, the communist philosophy will be set upon the straight path to the discovery and development of its proper ontology, without which no philosophy can be said to be complete or even to be a philosophy.

Meanwhile political democracy runs the danger, through professing no specific theory of knowledge, of being accused of holding the wrong one. There can be no avoidance of so fundamental a question as that of how we acquire the knowledge that we have. To ignore it is tantamount to insisting that no one theory is more valid than any other; which negation implies either, directly, a mentalism, or, indirectly, an irrationalism leading to a mentalism. That, on the other alternative, there is an epistemology compatible with democratic principles, and that this epistemology is that of realism, is a proposition set forth in part here.

5.

The Social Occasion for Recent Realism

THE FULL EXPLANATION OF ANY ITEM CONSISTS IN PLACING it in a logical system and in showing how it has arisen in history. The first part of the explanation exhibits its cause, the second its occasions. It follows that the cause of an item must remain the same always, whereas its occasion may vary throughout history. If one is thinking of something else while pumping up an automobile tire, and puts in eighty pounds instead of thirty, the tire will burst. If a car is driven a long while on a hot road, so that the air content of the tires expands by reason of the increase in its temperature, the tires will burst. These occurrences may be separated by months or years; they certainly are on different kinds of occasions; yet the fact remains that their causes are also the same: namely, the exertion of a pressure on the surface of a rubber fabric which that surface is not strong enough to bear.

Unfortunately, we find that from time to time, one kind of explanation is stressed to the neglect of the other. In the Middle Ages, for example, the explanation by cause was considered sufficient. Today, the explanation by occasion is often considered sufficient. Yet it follows from our description of explanation that neither occasion nor cause alone is sufficient but that both are required for every item to be explained. That this is a

useful caution, will become apparent to anyone who ex-
amines the question of method in the various studies,
for instance the social studies, which still lie outside the
field of exact science. The philosophers too are serious
offenders in this respect, since they usually argue merely
from the causal explanation, and consider occasions as
either belonging to the history of philosophy as a special
field, or as belonging to a topic lying outside the field of
philosophy.

The Marxist school of philosophy and economics
deems it sufficient to place an item in its historical context, without offering any explicit explanation of its logical place in a system. Marxists have shown with excellent clarity how types of philosophy are inevitably
associated with, reflect and are reflected by, corresponding
sorts of political government. For example, it has been
shown that subjective idealism is the philosophy associated with fascism. It has likewise been shown that
objective materialism is the philosophy associated with
communism. When the Marxists come, however, to
the question of what economic and political associations
the philosophy of realism has, they confess they are
puzzled. The commonest solution has consisted in
identifying realism with some sort of subjective idealism, and hence in condemning it as a fascist philosophy.
Such condemnation is hardly fair to realism, and could
only logically follow from a serious misunderstanding.

A close investigation into the original error which has
led to this conclusion reveals that realism has been limited by the Marxists to a variety of objective idealism, a
placing of the mind somehow outside the body and in
the world. Universals are thought to be mental entities
mysteriously floating about in the ether, and just as mys-

teriously constituting the reality of all being. It must be admitted that certain varieties of realism do lead to such a conclusion; but even at best this is a crude understanding of them. The identification of realism with objective idealism was for two reasons a natural enough error for the Marxists. Firstly, their own origins led straight back, at least in part, to Hegel and his school, and Hegelians could with some justice be accused of fostering such a philosophy. Secondly, the confining of explanation to that half which is in terms of occasion, or history, has led the Marxists astray in this respect as in others. Although realism is not limited to objective idealism, the latter can be defended on the grounds that the origins of ideas place no stigma on their being. The fact that universals are first known through the mind as ideas no more makes them into mental entities than the fact that chairs are first known through the mind as chairs makes them into mental chairs.

The Marxists are, as a matter of fact, wrong in supposing that merely because there appear to be no categories other than those of subjectivism and objectivism, realism, not being an objective affair like their own materialism, must, from the argument by exclusion of alternatives, be altogether subjective. Objective idealists will understand the assertion that the philosophy of realism is not limited to their variety. There are of course realistic elements in objective idealism, but to identify the two is absurd. Dialectical materialists admit that mechanistic materialists are materialists like themselves, but shrink from the thought that the difference between mechanism and dialectics is not highly important or in some respects crucial. And the same is true of the difference between objective idealism and realism.

Objective idealism talks about the world as frozen mind, but realism never does. For realism there is a logical order, a structure of being, which is known to the mind through objects but which is absolutely independent of the process of knowing. Certain thoroughgoing realists assert the same of values, that the logical order is an order of values, a hierarchy of affectability, which is known to the individual through sensation but which is absolutely independent of the process of sensation. There are many other important and closely related doctrines which are inevitably associated with the basic postulates of realism, but it will not be possible to enter into a discussion of these here. The relevant point to be considered is that the current critics of realism are justifiably voicing the age-long complaint against technical philosophy: what has it got to do with the price of eggs? Philosophers, as we have seen, are usually guilty of considering sufficient that explanation which places their metaphysical assumptions in a coherent system, and of overlooking the historical occasions which have given rise to such philosophy.

In the present day, which is witnessing tremendous political and economic upheavals, when the two philosophies of subjective idealism and dialectical materialism stand behind their respective political adherents, the fascists and the communists, it has well been asked: what is the social occasion for the rise of recent realism? Why has this particular philosophy grown into favor at this particular time? The importance of realism in recent times makes it a philosophy which cannot well be overlooked. Realism is represented by such names as Charles S. Peirce, G. E. Moore, G. Dawes Hicks, Bertrand Russell (in an early period, at least), A. N. Whitehead, G. Santayana, N. Hartmann, D. Parodi, and the American realists: Montague, Perry, and many others. There is a large and growing group of persons which admits that there is some justice in the Marxist demand that any current activity must be identified with its historic rôle, and which recognizes that even though this does not provide an exhaustive explanation it is a partial and a significant one, and should be seriously considered. This demand should be and must be satisfied.

When, however, we face the investigation of just what is the social occasion for the rise of recent realism, we learn at once that we have undertaken a task presenting many difficulties. It becomes obvious that the Marxists in their insistence on historical rather than historicological explanation have tended to read history in a special sense. The explanation of the social occasion for realism may have to wait until present-day realism has had its historical effect, and this may take a long while beyond our own lifetime. It is a notorious fact that the recognition and full effect of a philosophy has often to wait some years, decades, or even centuries, until after the philosophers themselves are dead. Thus the social occasion which prompted the writing of the philosophy may not be apparent to contemporaries of the philosophers themselves. The unity of theory and practice cannot be naively interpreted as the unity of present-day theory with present-day practice. Present-day theory may have a unity with future practice, present practice with previous theory. Thus realism today may have its practice in a future time, and the failure to discover any present-day practice for it should not lead (as indeed it has already mistakenly led) to the conclusion that realism is philosophizing in the void with no historical occasion whatsoever in operation.

It seems that the confusion of realism with ivory-tower philosophy can be eliminated if it can be shown that realism is clearly not an escape from reality but already has implications to and from the contemporary social scene. That realists may not as a group agree with the explanation offered here is not to the point. Realists are not in the habit of showing the political and economic connections of their doctrine, and moreover it must be claimed that on Marxist as well as on realist grounds the opinion of a philosopher as to the social occasion for his doctrines may or may not coincide with the true situation.

In the light of these difficulties, an hypothesis as to the social occasion for recent realism may with some temerity accordingly be set forth. Modern realists are for the most part members of the middle class, and they have been accused of being apologists for their class. They have been deemed escapists who have wished to retire into an unreal dream world which is of their own making and lacks any basis in the objective real world. But this charge is leveled only by those who confuse them with subjective idealists. Modern realists, of course, are members of the middle class; that much is true. But they are not concerned merely to save one economic group at the expense of others, and so they cannot be dismissed as apologists. A careful study of realists' writings reveals that they are not all concerned to save a given group of persons but rather a given group of accomplishments; these consist in certain truths and values which have been made actual through the labors of the middle class. The realists are renegades from the middle class in that they are willing to preserve those truths and values in any society which may arise. For instance, in a Marxist society the realists would find themselves clamoring for attention to such neglected facts as the intangible but nevertheless objective and real existence of ideal goals: the classless society and the withering away of the state. In a fascist society the realists (provided they were allowed to speak) would find themselves clamoring for attention to such neglected facts as the necessity of referring all judgments to objective, actual (i.e., in one sense material) conditions. In a fascist society the middle class as a class needs no apologists, but its special achievements do. In both societies the realists would have to stand for the possibility of discovering an independent truth which could be checked against objective fact but which would be independent of such fact.

The confusion of the defense of the middle class itself with the defense of certain truths and values which have been discovered by the middle class is due to the familiar confusion of occasion with cause. It does not seem possible to attribute to recent realism an economic cause, although it has most assuredly an economic occasion. The error of mistaking the occasion for the cause is common among literal and extreme Marxists, but is not to be laid to Marxism. The economic occasion for recent realism consists in the fact that certain realists, having observed the present-day political and economic upheaval and the imminence of radical change, fear for the preservation of certain middle class truths and values which they have come to hold essential for civilization. These truths and values are in great danger of being abandoned with the middle class, the baby so to speak thrown out with the bath. This situation the realists believe to be an intolerable one, since the actualization of significant truths and values has only come about by the hardest struggles. So they rise to the defense of what the middle class has accomplished and which appears to them to be independent of that class, achievements jeopardized by their identification with a single class to the unjustifiable exclusion of others.

The truths and values to which we have referred are represented in the sphere of social action by the political doctrine of democracy, and its associated liberties. The old individualistic liberalism has broken down, democracy has been threatened, and the new social democracy, based on the inclusion among the liberties of the right to a decent economic minimum for every individual (under which industrialism proves to be a social and not an individual affair), rests upon the establishment of a social liberalism. Only on the foundations of social liberalism does it appear possible for democracy to survive.

Such problems, their proper posing and solution, are of course not always articulate. Philosophies reflect and are reflected by actual conditions, yet the real purpose of realism may appear to some realists to be random. But what acts unconsciously and implicitly is as effective as what acts consciously and explicitly. Recent realists, therefore, represent the conscious or unconscious search for a valid philosophy which could furnish the endorsement necessary for social democracy. Such would appear to be the social occasion for the rise of recent realism.

Realism, it should be remembered, like any other set of abstract metaphysical principles, is absolutely independent of the occasions which call it forth. In so far as the same realistic postulates are adopted by realists throughout historical time, there is no difference between one realism and another. This means that realism and the temporal order are separable. Nevertheless, the exhibition of how and why realism arises at any given date and place is illustrative both of the workings of the temporal order and of the exploration of some special implications of the realistic philosophy. Thus when we comprehend that realism can serve as a justification for those achievements of bourgeois democracy which are worth saving past the narrow interests of the bourgeois class itself, we are learning more than practical politics; we are learning that an age-long and important philosophy can and must be understood to be relevant to the most urgent of contemporary problems. And, finally, when we learn that social democracy and its united front of democratic parties rests upon the sound basis of metaphysical realism, we are learning more than theoretical philosophy; we are learning that metaphysics is not idle speculation but rather a vitally important topic carrying with it implications to every field of actual practice. An understanding of the social occasion for the rise of recent realism is equally important for society and for the furtherance of the philosophy of realism.

6.

Individualism Under the Great Cultures

The Individual and Society

THE IMPORTANCE OF INDIVIDUALISM IN NEGATIVE DEMOCracy has raised the question of whether individualism can exist at all in positive social democracy, or whether its omission would not destroy the basis of that democracy we have come to know in practice. We have always associated individualism with democracy, yet individualism has existed under other political systems and even in other cultures. It will aid in the understanding of what the rôle of individualism in a positive social democracy could be, to consider it in other social contexts and with a broader setting than that of contemporary political involvements. The object of this chapter, then, is to study the relation of individualism to the great cultures.

It has long been the custom to regard societies as changing in some cyclical or evolutionary manner. But despite this common observation it has also been the custom to regard the individual as a fixed and absolute unit, a kind of social atom which is capable of combining in any number of ways to form widely different kinds of societies but which remains itself incapable of alteration. There is no reason to believe this, since nothing else in the actual world defies change in such a manner. Certainly the physical individual is to a large (though not exclusive) extent unaffected by the social environment, but at higher levels the change in the individual is clearly observable. Briefly, individualism does not replace communalism in one culture and become destroyed by it in another. It rather survives in all cultures, but only by taking its form from the culture in which it exists.

In order to ascertain the true place of the individual in society, it will be necessary to bear in mind that individualism is by its nature a relative affair. There is no such thing as an absolutely self-sufficient individual; even in abstraction the notion does not carry sufficient validity to be of any service. Every person can be considered an individual to the extent to which he uniquely advances or delays the attainment of the purpose of society. It may be flatly declared that man is a social animal, and that he functions properly only as an integral part of society. By society here is meant an unlimited society, and not any narrowly understood social group. Of course the individual's participation in society must not be understood, either, in any crude physical sense. For most persons participation means proximity and nothing more. But it has been pointed out time and again that the great leaders, such men as artists, saints, and even in some cases scientists, in order to perform their social function find it necessary to conduct their lives practically as hermits. The inventor of the Heaviside calculus, an instrument which has been of inestimable advantage in industry and therefore of benefit to society, was almost completely a hermit. There are thousands of examples. For many, the love of and the labor for society is only made possible by complete social withdrawal. But this does not alter the fact that man is a social animal.

The social nature of individual man is not a new discovery. Indeed some traditions in the history of actual social theory have leaned over backwards in the effort to give due credit to the social function of the individual. Such emphasis has occasionally gone too far. The prejudice of subjective idealism in favor of the relations between man and God and between man and man, to the exclusion of man's recognition of the natural world as a thing entirely independent of him and of his ambitions, has hindered the human adventure not a little. The Greek preference for the "pure" investigation of nature has resulted in many discoveries inadvertently proved to be of use for society. Roentgenology, which has been so beneficial to human beings, was not a product of the so-called human sciences. Man exists at other levels besides the social, and his sociality is a fact neither more nor less important than the fact of his physical, biological or psychological being. It is not possible to place man in relation to society without a proper comprehension of what lies below man as an organization and a guess at what may lie above society.

The viewpoint that man is the servant of society, or rather that the true function of the individual is to serve society, has awaited proper formulation because the organizational hierarchy of existence has never been properly understood. A number of plants are required to support an animal and a number of animals are required to support a human being and a number of human beings are required to support a society. But what

a society or a number of societies supports surpasses
present knowledge. It is here that even conjecture ends
and we must confess our total ignorance. Presumably
there is an organization, even an organism, higher than
society; but what this could mean, except foolishness,
no one can say. The advancement of knowledge by
extrapolation of ratios, we may painfully remind ourselves, is what brought about the mediaeval belief in
the hierarchy of angels. It is therefore at the point of
society that we must stop, with the justifiable conclusion
that there must be a purpose for society, since the existence of anything without some sort of purpose cannot
be asserted, yet with the further conclusion that we assuredly do not yet know what that purpose is.

There are few alternatives in the history of philosophy
to the view that the purpose of man is to serve society.
Aristotle's definition of man as a "rational animal," the
description of man, more of a stigma than a definition,
as a "featherless biped," or the charge that he is "an ape
that has grown weary of climbing," are all classifications
which rely on some one subsidiary function and do not
define in terms of purpose. The teleological character of
the social is admitted even by those extreme individual-
ists who deny the reality of society. For even while
they tell us that society is not an organization but merely
a collection of individuals they are ready to admit that
the worth of a person is strongly influenced if not entirely determined by the value of his relations with other
individuals. And since it is clear that the organizational
series of scientific levels is pointed upward in degree of
complexity and scope, we may safely conclude that the
purpose of man consists in the service of society. There
are of course a number of ways in which this function

may be performed, involving more or less actual participation in society, all the way from complete submergence of the individual in the social to what Toynbee has described as individual "withdrawal-and-return."

We may next ask whether the decision as regards the form of the individual's service to society is entirely in the hands of the individual himself. The answer to this question is that to a certain extent at least it is. In any given society the range of variation of individual activity (speaking only of those who are of actual benefit to society) is enormous. However, it is not with this range of variation and its causes that this work is primarily concerned, but with the extent to which the individual's participation in and service to society is out of his hands. For it must be apparent that to a large extent it is a matter over which he can exercise only a limited amount of control.

In what way and to what extent is the activity of the individual dictated by the society of which he is a member? In order to examine this question, we must turn to an analysis of the culture types, and to the further question of what they specifically demand of the individual. The demands of the cultures are by no means uniform or on the same level. They differ in ways which make the comparison of the individual as he varies from culture to culture almost impossible. Nevertheless, since this is a question which has been largely overlooked, it will bear some investigation.

The Four Types of Culture

Nobody knows just what cultures are, or how they rise and fall. Various efforts have been made to define them and to trace their adventures, but none of these efforts has met with any astonishing success. Vico, Spengler, Toynbee, are only a few of the illustrious names of those who have labored at this task. The principal results of their work consist in the observation that civilizations do rise and fall, and that certain predominating ideas govern in some mysterious manner. Yet their theories remain largely affairs of conjecture, interesting but for the most part fruitless. Nevertheless, they are not entirely fruitless, and the suggestions contained in them constitute whatever leads we have toward further investigation.

The term "culture" for the purposes of this study will be given a definition in terms of logic rather than psychology. The cultural anthropologists who judge culture to be more basic than philosophy, and who consider philosophy merely as one of the aspects or activities of a culture, are speaking of explicit philosophy as it fares in the hands of professional philosophers. By such an understanding, primitive cultures, for instance, would be said to have no philosophy, while philosophy entire would be limited to its manifestations in civilized societies. This view of philosophy is a hopeless one, but, fortunately for the fate of reason in the world, also a false one. For every society has a philosophy—we may say *is* a philosophy—and this remains true even though in some societies it is not known. The primitive cultures do not cease to represent certain metaphysical postulates simply because all persons in them continue unaware of the fact. A philosophy in this sense, then, is the accepted dominant ontology of a people. Implicit philosophy is the ontological structure of the natural world. The accepted dominant ontology of a people is their theory, which need not be consciously held, of what this ontological structure of the natural world is. Thus implicit philosophy is prior to all forms of culture, and the philosophy of a given culture is ontologically prior to anything else in it.

However prior a philosophy may be, there is yet a second factor which operates in the determination of a culture. The accepted ontology is the cause of a culture, but the environment is its occasion. An Eskimo and an American plains Indian may adopt the same ontology, but experience with the varying environment forces one to wear much and hunt fish and the other to wear little and hunt deer. The environment, however, includes much more than the merely physical. It also includes whatever is available socially as an influence—contacts temporal or spatial with other cultures. Thus the epistemological sphere of knowledgeable acquaintance with the actual world is the modifying factor in the application of an accepted dominant ontology.

Bearing these two conditions in mind, the accepted dominant ontology and the total modifying environment, we may now define a culture as the given set of customs, tools, and institutions at which a people arrive by virtue of their acceptance of a certain theory of implicit philosophy, plus whatever modifications are made necessary by the exigencies of actual circumstances at a specific date and place. Culture thus consists in the applied deductions of philosophy. Integrated cultures are small sets of logical premises from which are drawn all possible implications allowable under the circumstances. The diversity of cultural traits in this connection is accounted for by understanding them to be merely applied deductions which in the course of practice have taken to leading a life of their own.

The classical habit of setting up categories for the great cultures in the hope that these categories will prove to be the true ones is a method guilty of the fallacy of oversimplification. Comte and Frazer have made absolute divisions between cultures, but these divisions do not stand the test of close examination. The method chosen here is rather one of distinguishing properties which are possessed in more or less degree by all of the great cultures. The cultures are divided according as one or another of these properties dominates. It is necessary to add that no actual cultures are being described here, but properties which actual cultures possess in more or less degree. The properties to be examined are the primitive, the martial, the religious and the scientific. As operative in the great cultures, they will be examined under the following classes: (1) animism, (2) materialism, (3) spiritualism, and (4) scientism.

Animistic cultures are those in which neither theories nor practices are enabled to rise above the basic subsistence problem. The divisions of labor are anything but distinct, because there is no other motive for action except the increase of the fertility of crops and herds, and the sound preservation of the human stock. Thus the only cultural traits which are known to possess universal distribution among primitives are those of animism and exogamy. Life is governed by the belief in the forces of nature which can be invoked and propitiated. The chief method of invocation and propitiation is imitative magic, for instance, dancing for rain. A good example of the animistic type of culture is the Polynesian group in the French Society Islands.

Material cultures are distinguished by the surrender to the dominant theory of rank materialism, that the sensible objects which are actually presented to us are alone real. The gods propitiated are no longer subsistence deities but rather gods of war, for instance Marduk and Mars. The motive for action here has risen above bare subsistence to the ownership of materials for their own sake, for instance as these are productive of pleasurable sensations. The pattern is one in which the behavior of war dominates, and the culture is planned for material aggrandizement. This chiefly takes the form of the conquest of other peoples and nations. An example of this type of culture is the civilization of ancient Assyria.

The third culture is that of spiritualism, in which the dominant theory is of the religious type. By this is meant that actual materials are scorned in favor of some form of superior reality which is non-present: either a life after death, or a realm of essence of which this actual world is considered to be but a shadow. The gods propitiated are those who make it possible to rise above or survive the earthly life. Attention to the ugliness, evil, and contradictions of actuality have occasioned a dialectical emphasis on that pattern of behavior which will avoid them altogether and with them much that is actually worthy. Thus holiness and asceticism are cultivated to the exclusion of other activities. Examples of religious culture are Christianity and Buddhism.

The fourth culture is that of scientism, and it is of the realistic type. In this variety of culture, the dominant theory is the primary reality of laws as these are found operative or capable of operating in this actual world. Life is governed by the idea that the discovery of natural conditions will both satisfy interest in the search for truth and lead to the improvement of living conditions. The chief motive for action is inquiry, and the chief aim of inquiry is the knowledge of natural laws. The pattern is one in which the behavior of investigation dominates, and the culture is planned for the increase of natural knowledge. An example of this type of culture is that of modern Europe and America.

It will be evident at once that these categories over-lap, and that no actual cultures are being described. This point must be insisted on in order to avoid error in interpretation. Perhaps no culture is either purely the one or the other, yet that is no argument against the validity of the categories. We never find atoms and motion, or wood and trees, apart, yet it is useful to dis-tinguish between them. In this connection, some dis-cussion of the contrast and comparison of the cultures will be in order.

First of all, the types of cultures are in no wise to be understood as a chronological procession. The order of animistic, materialistic, spiritualistic and scientific is not the absolute order in which the great cultures have been born and have advanced, though some relative chronological progression is intended. Roughly, ani-mism precedes materialism, materialism precedes spirit-ualism, and spiritualism precedes scientism. But the progression is dialectic rather than serial. The categories overlap severely; there are rapid advances and sharp re-treats or retrogressions; and there are many other di-vergences from a strict serial progression. For instance, the Apache Indians of the North American southwest were primitives containing large elements of the martial-materialistic culture. Nazi Germany marks a return to the martial-materialistic on the part of a culture which had already been dedicated to the scientific. Other totalitarian regimes exist in countries which were not markedly scientific, e.g., Spain, Turkey. There is more at issue in the fascist movement than is contained in the denial of science. The late and feeble effort of some states to assume the modern Western dress of democracy and science has not concealed their deeper martial-materialistic character, which emerges into the open once the pretense to liberalism is frankly abandoned.

The four types of cultures evidently hold to the principle that a certain kind of activity will best serve the accepted dominant ontology. The materialistic and the spiritualistic have to do with a primary reality which is resident in this world or in a presupposed otherworld. They assume the premise of attainable goals, and serve these with attitudes as much as with practices. The attitudes are not allowed to be relaxed. The animistic and the scientific, on the other hand, although equally governed by the accepted dominant ontology, have to do rather with the assumed premise of an efficacious practical activity which furthers the progress toward an unattainable goal, and which thus has to be repeated at frequent periodic intervals. It is remarkable that the spiritualistic and materialistic cultures set themselves attainable goals, whereas the animistic and the scientific have approachable but unattainable ones. But most important is the fact that all four cultures are primarily grounded in varying theories of reality.

To sum up the argument thus far, we have defined the individual in terms of his purpose as the servant of society, and we have raised the point that individualism is not absolute but relative, and that the direction of individualism is to a considerable extent governed by the type of the social culture in which the individual happens to find himself. We then set up a classification of cultures, our criterion being the acceptance of a dominant ontology. We shall next turn to investigate the specific relations between the cultures selected for study and the individuals who are members of those cultures. If individualism is always a standard of greatness, no individual being considered great who has not in some way set himself apart from the remainder of society, then how is such individualism affected by having to exist in one or another of the cultures?

Cultural Demands on the Individual

We shall begin by posing another problem. What ethical question does each culture ask of the individual? The answer, as we shall see, is different in each instance. Individual morality is largely a matter of what the culture demands. But for any one of the cultures it is true that there is no one-to-one relation between the contemporary estimation of greatness and greatness itself. Some men are immediately recognized as having made an outstanding contribution to society, as for instance Pericles, Dickens, Rubens, while others are not, as for instance Keats, Cervantes, Marx. It is not always immediately evident to a culture just who its leaders are, because a culture is a whole culture and not that part of it observable at any one time. There is nevertheless a definite relationship between culture and individual greatness.

(1) The animistic cultures ask the ethical question of the individuals in them, "How communal are you?"

The outstanding individual is not one who departs from the accepted norm but rather one who most brilliantly executes the traditional pattern of life. The communal life is, so to speak, so tight, and so highly organized, that any individual who revolts from it or who wishes to change the inherited order of its customs and institutions is *ipso facto* no longer a member of that society. He is outcast, and may no longer participate in the life of his community; he must leave or else die for his pains. He is not considered at the time, or even later, anything but a degenerate member of the society. He is regarded simply as one who was not strong enough to meet the demands which are put upon the individual by the extremely complex set of practices which are characteristic of the primitive culture.

It has long been the habit among certain anthropologists to regard a high degree of communal life as a limitation of animistic cultures, and certainly, with regard to their failure to achieve the special kinds of basic material advance which should be demanded of every society, the judgment is correct. But the anthropologists tend to go to one extreme or another in a rough general way, and conclude either that communalism retards social advance and keeps it at a very low stage, or else that self-sufficiency is enough of an attainment and would only be lost by any efforts at progress. There is, however, a third way in which the highly communal life of the primitives can be regarded. It will be recalled that society is an organization higher than individual man in the series. Since every activity occasions the manifestation of certain values, the higher the activity the higher the values manifested. Consequently, certain values are apprehended by group activities which can be achieved in no other way. The individual alone is powerless to apprehend them. But by his participation in the social life, the individual is privileged to participate in social values. To witness the Hopi snake-dance or the Navajo ceremonial is to understand what a profound satisfaction it is for a primitive to be able to participate in the values which are made possible for him by his clan. The obvious emotions can be matched by nothing similar in cultures which are in other respects higher.

It is logical, then, in such a highly organized social life as that of the primitives that the question, "How communal are you?" should be the test of individual greatness. Whosoever thinks it a paradox to assert that the individual in an animistic society is being most individual when he is most social, must have been led by the implicit acceptance of the standards of his own culture into misunderstanding the primitive situation. Let it not be supposed that great communality is not an outstanding personal triumph for the individual. Few are able ever to attain it, even among the primitives where so many are contestants for the honor. When society makes tremendous demands upon the individual, as it assuredly does in the best of animistic cultures, there are few individuals who are able to measure up to what is expected of them. These are marked men indeed, and they are usually singled out for whatever honors the societies have to offer by way of distinction.

(2) The materialistic cultures ask the ethical question of the individuals in them, "How well do you fight?"

The outstanding individual here is asked literally to step apart from his fellows and candidly to assume the rôle of leadership. There is exaggerated leadership of the few and the sheepish following of the many. This is what we today call a "war-time basis." The material cultures are in certain degrees higher than the primitive cultures, but in other respects they are not. They are certainly not as highly organized, although they appear to be so because their aims and ambitions are much simpler. The individual is asked to smother whatever personal feelings he may happen to experience in the interests of working toward a common goal. The means employed generally consist of the wide conquest and subjection of neighboring peoples by war, since this is the most efficient way of attaining the desired goal, namely the possession of material wealth. The great individual must not falter; he must neither show nor have compassion for those he commands and those he conquers. His men must be driven, and his enemies must be suppressed, whatever the cost in human lives on either side. Thus heroism and self-sacrifice in war become the highly regarded virtues, and everything else in the culture is taken as merely furthering the highly simplified end. "Men exist for war, and women for the amusement of the warrior, all else is folly," said Nietzsche. Such is the martial view.

The materialistic cultures at first glance appear to be highly organized, just as the animistic cultures are. But first glances here as elsewhere are apt to be misleading. All is not high organization which meets the eye as wholes. The animistic cultures are highly organized; the materialistic cultures are highly regimented. But regimentation is not organization; the cultural facts are clearly different. The primitive organization is one in which the individual reaches his highest point of individuality by being more than anyone else a good member of the social group. The martial regimentation, on the other hand, is one in which the individual surrenders his rights in favor of the common pursuit of a goal which is expected to be of benefit not to the social group as a whole but to each individual. "United we stand, divided we fall," is the common cry; and there is no other bond. The martial regimentation is, so to speak, a thieves' compact, a quondam surrender of individual rights which is at least supposed to be terminable. The social contract is entered into in the materialistic culture out of necessity and not because of the sustaining and permanent benefits of the social life.

We have the opportunity of witnessing the materialistic type of culture at work in our own time, in the rule of the Nazis in Germany. What has been said applies as much to Germany today as to ancient Assyria. The individual benefits to be derived from participation in the social life of a materialistic culture are doubtful, because the combination formed out of surrendered individual rights is difficult to destroy. The division of the war-won booty never takes place; there is no parting of the ways. And there is meanwhile no worthwhile attainment in the social life of the group.

(3) The spiritualistic cultures ask the ethical question of the individuals in them, "How devout are you?"

The outstanding individual in this type of culture is the one who leads the most holy life. In this type of culture there is regimentation, too, but there is also high organization. The common end is the avoidance of any important actual life which might be based on the reality of sense experience, in favor of the pursuit of an otherworldly existence. The religious societies expect their individuals to be members of one vast salvation army marching away from actuality and toward a goal which lies beyond finite human life. The expectation of conduct put upon the individual by society is tremendous, but not because any great values are to be manifested for the individuals by the social perfection of organization. On the contrary, the whole aim is the avoidance of concrete values, and the achievement of a common denial of life. There is a leadership, but not the absolute leadership of a materialistic society. There is rather a leadership the absoluteness of whose autocracy is cushioned by a hierarchy of sub-leaders descending in importance right down to the laity. The Church's supreme leader speaks, presumably, only to God and to divines lesser than himself. These speak to others beneath them, until the word of God is finally conveyed to the common people. Of such is the kingdom of heaven.

The ceremony is presented to the common view of actual flesh-and-blood leaders who lead their actual flesh-and-blood flock away from the means of attaining anything actual and to the immediate end of the devout life which looks toward a superior world, generally in which enjoyment is more permanent than anything the poor senses could afford, anyway. The great individual here is one who goes the whole way in devotion, so much so that he is forced to withdraw altogether from the communion of the group in favor of an absolutistic isolationist policy. He is the incarnate individual, though he may not think of it in these terms, and there is no other one except the creator of the universe. The hierarchy of means and ends whereby intermediate ends become themselves means for the attainment of a more remote end, is really too social a doctrine for the spiritualistic cultures ever to accept.

What is substituted for this doctrine is a religious ritual as prescribed by a militant church, a ritual which acts as the lame survival of a primitive, efficacious, practical activity which is supposed to further the progress toward the chosen goal. The fact is that in some respects the religious cultures are unsuccessful attempts to repeat on a higher scale the pattern of the primitive cultures. The interest in subsistence is well-hidden in the spiritualistic cultures, and sometimes, for instance, takes the disinterested form of prayers for the abatement of the lumbago of a maiden aunt. The animistic subsistence gods sometimes hear prayers for rain, but the notorious fact remains that even the gods of the great spiritualistic cultures refuse to be permanently propitiated. Lumbago is after all lumbago. And the individual, who is expected to extract what wry solace he can from such an interim socialism composed of a myriad of self-interests, suffers accordingly.

As a representative of the spiritualistic cultures, we may choose the Catholic Church. Its leaders have been great leaders; we may cite the names of such men as St. Francis, St. Thomas Aquinas, St. Augustine, and Jesus. Their contributions to society, whether in the form of examples of lives lived, or in the written rational presentations of theology, or in both, are tremendous because they tend to reach beyond the culture which produced them. But its lesser leaders are hardly leaders at all, as anyone who is familiar with the minor clergy can testify, and there are far more of them. As to the lay individuals who make up the vast body of the culture group, whether their sacrifice was worth while or not cannot be recorded. As yet nobody has written back from beyond the grave to report the difference in rewards between the portions of the heathen and the true believer.

(4) We come to examine the effect of the last of our culture types upon the individual. The scientific cul-

tures ask the ethical question of the individuals in them, "How puzzled are you?"

The outstanding individual in this type of culture is the one who is most anxious methodically to investigate what the whole business of existence is all about. The criterion of individual greatness is the degree of self-abnegating curiosity of the individual and the extent to which he is willing and even anxious to rely upon the negative checking of experimentation of his guesses as to what entities and processes go to make up the natural conditions whereby the actual world can exist at all. In this type of culture there has been something borrowed from the spiritualistic cultures, inasmuch as the goal is set of the attainment of truths which extend beyond the immediate finite world of sense experience. There is the difference however, that no otherworldly goal is desired, but rather a continually improving actual world of the future, wherein the conditions for and of society are expected to be, by virtue of the truths discovered, rendered better and better. An actual future, in this world, of generations of social groups to come is substituted for a disembodied otherworld of the future.

This change of goals puts the scientific cultures into touch also with the animistic cultures. Both tend to elevate the social life as being of more value to the individual than the individual life itself is for him, with the difference that the scientific cultures are not willing to remain fixed, constant and stable, like the primitives, but want to go forward along the chosen lines toward greater and greater benefits for society. Thus the scientific culture provides the individual with a wholly personal way of life, set aside for the most part from the public life, but offering to this different kind of privacy the satisfaction of an actual service to public ends. It has a remote goal, but an actual one, and it contains within it at least the promise of an integrated apprehension of achievable social values which are forever to be attained.

Individualism as defined for the scientific cultures does not mean by its puzzlement the confusion of vagueness, insanity, or defeat. These are highly specific forms of individualism, for there is nothing more specific than the particular errors into which psychotic thinking is driven. But they are not scientific in the sense that they are not seeking *methodically* to discover laws, and the rational-empirical or scientific method of research is practically definitive for the scientific cultures. We are further unhappy in having to date only one example of the scientific culture, whereas there have been countless numbers of the others. Moreover, our society is far from being complete of its kind; the scientific attitude is accepted only by some few persons, and by them only in certain fields. We too are living in the midst of that scientific example, and so we have as yet no finished product to offer for comparison. We know little enough of its faults, and we are very likely to overstress its virtues. As examples of the great individuals of our culture we have to offer any number, but of the greatest, certainly such men as Galileo, Newton, and Einstein. What characterizes their individuality is the absence of self-interest, the assiduity of their unrelenting pursuit of knowledge, and their constant wonder. These are our great individuals; can we honestly deny them a common likeness? The saints of the scientific culture are those to whom both pure knowledge and its practical application are means toward the mediate end of social welfare.

Conclusions

We may return now to our original question, namely, how is individualism as a standard of greatness affected by the participation of the individual in one or another of the great cultures. The various threads of the argument, as these emerge from our examination of the attempts of the individuals to supply in superlative measure what is demanded of them by the cultures in which they happen to exist, will lead to the general conclusions which bring this chapter to an end.

Contemporary individualism rests upon the extent of the freedom of the individual from social restraint. How free is the individual from the necessity of participating in social activities? That is the modern test for the degree of individualism in a given society. Looking back over the cultures we have surveyed, however, we are able to detect an entirely different criterion. There can be little doubt that the order in which we have listed the cultures also represents a progression, however slight, in civilization. From primitive cultures through martial and religious to scientific may be a direction indicating a loss of certain values, but from the broad point of view it is also a direction indicating a total gain.

The criterion for this gain is that of increase in awareness. We live in a tremendous universe whose enormity is the first thing apparent to animistic man, as he huddles together with his kind and seeks to maintain his existence. He attempts to propitiate in the name of his social group the natural powers which are so obviously stronger than his weak efforts. Thus he is aware only of the values of his social group. For materialistic man his culture has been enough to ward off the evil forces in his world; he has built strong houses which are capable of withstanding the elements, and he has weapons which make him more than the equal of wild animals. He thus is free to look about him, and when he does so he beholds his neighbors' society and sees that it is good, and so endeavors to take possession of it. Materialistic man has thus extended awareness to include the neighboring social groups.

The horizon of spiritualistic man is even wider than that of materialistic man, but he is still anthropocentric. The conquests of materialistic man are either just over or just about to begin; and in either case there is a realization that the similarity of peoples and the bond between them is not exhausted by their propinquity. There are other bases for the general human alliance. Spiritualistic man is thus aware not only of the values of his group, like animistic man, nor only of the values of the neighboring groups, like materialistic man, but of the values of all humanity—the entire social world. With the transition from spiritualistic to scientific man there is a sharp break. Spiritualistic man has carried anthropocentrism as far as it will go. Scientific man, however, is no longer anthropocentric; he is ontocentric. The progression from animistic to spiritualistic has welded the social forces together; now whatever is of benefit to one social group perforce has to be extended to the whole of humanity, if all the gains made are not to be lost. Scientific man is aware that there is no cleavage but on the contrary a very strong connection between material culture and general social welfare. He is also aware that there is no cleavage between human society and the natural world. He is thus once more aware of nature, but as a friendly and not as an unfriendly

force, and he has found a technique which can execute
the double movement of investigating the conditions of
nature and advancing material culture. This technique
is the scientific method. From the viewpoint of cultural
anthropology we may describe the scientific method as
the civilized way of propitiating the forces of nature.

The animistic man relies on ritual, the materialistic
man on concerted action, and the spiritualistic man on
passive sensitivity, but the scientific man combines the
ritual of method with a concerted action based on a
passionate although sure sensitivity. Strictly speaking,
animistic man is social, materialistic man individual,
spiritualistic man both social and individual, but scientific man neither, exclusively. For the individual, the
progress is from inorganic organization to plant aware of
little, to animal aware of more, to animistic man aware
of his culture group, to materialistic man aware of other
culture groups, to spiritualistic man aware of all culture
groups, to scientific man endeavoring to be aware of that
vast totality of nature in which all of the culture groups
are imbedded as integral parts.

The individual as a unit in society is deeply affected
by a change in the accepted dominant ontology; he is
also deeply affected by any change in the degree of awareness of his social group. The effect of the culture group
upon the kind of individualism which the individual
within it displays, or is capable of displaying, is tremendous and all-enveloping. In fact it may be bluntly asserted that the criterion of greatness of the individual
varies directly with the aim of the culture of which he
is a part. Cultures appreciate outstanding individuals
sooner or later. But no individual can change his culture more than a very small extent. Moreover, no

culture thanks any individual in it for challenging its fundamental premises, and by fundamental here is meant premises which are so deeply held that they are not even consciously known. The advantage in this regard which the scientific culture has over other cultures is not that such a challenge is condoned, but that it is at least made possible.

The relation of individualism to the cultural life is hardly understood today. We tend to accept either individualism or socialism as a good and to reject the other as an evil. Other cultures than our own would be hard put to it to grasp such an attitude. We tend to admire individualism and to regard any social obligations as necessary intrusions. For scientific man, these social activities are painful duties whose minimal performance is a grudging payment he must make for his individual freedom. But when the primitive, for instance, takes part in the social life of his group, it is the enjoyment of a privilege and not merely the fulfillment of an obligation. Those who have witnessed the dances of the Tewa Indians of the New Mexico pueblos will appreciate what tremendous values are apprehended by the individual through his participation in the communal life, values unobtainable in any other way.

Whether individualism is to be regarded as a good or as an evil depends wholly upon the state of the society in which that individualism is to be assayed. Individualism is destroyed by a declining communal life striving to hold on; and in this kind of society it must be considered an evil. It is, on the other hand, an asset in a growing communal life striving for still further gains, since every individual achievement is held to be an advance for the community. The only reason why individualism is having such difficulties in getting the proper official recognition in Soviet Russia is because that country has not yet firmly and sufficiently established the communal life. When the communal life does find a firm basis we may be sure that there will be a place in it for individualism without the presence of a conflict. For it is the pressure of outside enemies which forces the development of martial elements in Russia today, as the Hittites and Babylonians forced full militarization upon the Assyrians.

The primitive may be said to have the proper communal life, but this has been possible only in a very small society and at the expense of much that the later cultures have cherished. Nobody yet has even envisaged what it would mean to have the kind of communal life which primitives enjoy, established at the level of civilization and with the tremendous populations which we have today. Fifth century Athens was only a faint adumbration of what a communal civilized society could be, a dim suggestion and nothing more. The chief problem of democracy in our time seems to be to widen the framework of the communal life in the scientific culture in such a way that it will include the values achieved by the other cultures. The communal life of civilization must be broadened and then tightened; it must include and embrace without destroying recent achievements of scientific culture. A world communal life, which could include individualism and the pursuit of pure as well as applied science while yet maintaining the high organization of its sociality, staggers the imagination. It would be a civilization which would dwarf anything that had ever gone before. In the doctrine of positive democracy we are endeavoring to discover the theoretical basis for such a society.

7.

Scientific Method in Politics

The Search for Science

IN THE LAST CHAPTER WE NOTED THE RELATION BETWEEN individualism and the great cultures in an effort to sound out the implications of the problem of individualism for democracy. In this chapter we shall take our approach from an altogether different point of view. We are throwing as much light as we can upon the ideal nature of democracy; but our remarks hitherto have been directed toward its constitution. Now we want to ask, "What is the ideal method of attaining democracy?" It must be immediately recognized that the scientific method is the ideal method of attaining anything which is susceptible to its treatment. In those fields in which scientific method has been correctly applied, the successes which have resulted have exceeded everyone's wildest hopes. Unfortunately, however, the application has not always been all that it should be. The common practice in some fields has been to ape the scientific method as employed in the highly successful science of physics. But the peculiarities of physics have led to a mistaken imitation of its postulates and conclusions in non-physical fields, and the result in many cases has been little more than nonsense. It is therefore wise, before suggesting that politics become a science, and that scientific method be applied to the political field, to set forth as briefly as possible the nature of science and of the scientific method in the abstract.

What is science? Let us seek an answer among the suggestions which have been put forward recently by scientists and the philosophers of science. We shall see that some of these proposals are invalid, and thus have to dismiss them, but we shall also find some which are valid, and of the latter we must endeavor to formulate our own solution.

We may begin with the definition offered by a mathematical physicist, Professor P. W. Bridgman of Harvard. He defines science in terms of the procedure of the scientist, a subjective interpretation. "In general, [he says] we mean by any concept nothing more than a set of operations; the concept is synonymous with the corresponding set of operations." [1] In other words, scientific concepts are merely symbols or convenient signs standing for certain physical operations. For example, when we say "three" we are indicating nothing more than the fact that we have counted, or can count, three objects. And when we say "gravitation" we are indicating nothing more than the fact that we have dropped, or can drop, some body, or, more broadly, that bodies can be dropped. This theory allows no objective validity to scientific laws. Indeed the subjective character of Professor Bridgman's conception is seen clearly by him. He tells us that "the nature of our thinking mechanism essentially colors any picture that we can form of na-

[1] P. W. Bridgman, The Logic of Modern Physics (New York, 1928), p. 5.

ture," [2] and that "from the operational point of view it is meaningless to attempt to separate 'nature' from 'knowledge of nature.' " [3]

This is the view which is known today as positivism. One of the founders of logical positivism, Professor Wittgenstein of Vienna and Cambridge University has seen that positivism is involved in subjective idealism or solipsism, the theory that the mind of the individual actually creates his entire world, and he does not reject it. [4]

From the position of Professor Bridgman, the objective agreement which is achieved by scientists is impossible to explain. Science is left with no objective world for subject matter and must rest content with the behavior of scientists. But behaviorism, the study of behavior, which is a branch of psychology, has failed even to account for the whole of psychology; why should we accept it as adequate to account for the whole of science? We might watch a scientist working for hours in his laboratory, but if we did not know that he was a scientist and if he did not tell us what he was trying to do, we would never be able to understand what he was doing. It is clear that although an opinion such as Bridgman's be expressed, it is not deeply held, nor, what is more to the point, followed by any scientist. Professor Wittgenstein has proved more logical and inexorable in pursuing to their conclusions the implications of his premises. As has been noted many times in the history of philosophy, subjective idealism is finally irrefutable. If we choose to believe that our minds have created

[2] Ibid., p. xi.
[3] Ibid., p. 62.
[4] Ludwig Wittgenstein, Tractatus Logico-Philosophicus (London, 1933).

everything we feel and know of the external world, that, so to speak, the world is our own, then there can be none to say us nay. So without envy we shall leave Wittgenstein literally to his own devices and pass on to the next definition of science.

The next definition we have to examine is that offered by Professor Morris R. Cohen. He says, "In turning to the sciences I emphasize their method rather than their results. For, in an age of scientific expansion, not only are the methods the more permanent features of the sciences, but the supposed results are often merely popularized conventions, utterly misleading to all those who do not know the processes by which they are obtained." [5] Earlier, in the eighteenth century, Linnaeus, the botanist, had asserted the same position. "All the real knowledge, which we possess," he wrote, "depends on method . . ." [6] The definition of science as scientific method has at least the merit of being more objective than those of Bridgman and Wittgenstein, and of granting more objective validity to the world. Scientific method is something more than a set of operations; it is a definite method, susceptible of abstract formulation and available to all who choose to learn its nature and to follow it. It is more certain and dependable than the random, wayward and inscrutable behavior of the scientists, when that behavior is expected to be self-explanatory. We know that scientific method stands independent of any scientist or group of scientists, that it can never be lost or destroyed, and that it yields results which are gratifying.

[5] Morris R. Cohen, *Reason and Nature* (4th ed. New York, 1932), p. x.
[6] Quoted in W. C. D. Dampier-Whetham, *Cambridge Readings in the Literature of Science* (Cambridge, 1928), p. 188.

Yet even here we cannot stop, content that we have found the proper definition. For it is just the little independent validity which is granted to science by means of this definition which demonstrates its insufficiency. For by the conventional definition, a method is a procedure, a *means* toward an end and *not* an end in itself. So then we must ask Professor Cohen and ourselves: what is the end which the method of science is to accomplish? Science, to put the matter bluntly, is the method *of accomplishing what?* But Professor Cohen has already admitted that scientific method is expected to get results. He is, however, properly suspicious of them, and hastens to assert that "dead or detached results lend themselves to the mythology of popular science, and ignorance of method leads to the view of science as a new set of dogmas to be accepted on the authority of a new set of priests called scientists." [7]

But this is where we must be wary. Cohen has played the old trick on us of showing the preference for one alternative over another, with the hidden assumption that the possibilities are exhausted by the two alternatives. By comparing the method of science with its "dead or detached results," he has made us see the advisability of accepting the definition of method. If this were the only choice, we would have been guided right. But there remains yet another. That is to say, we may attempt to determine the direction in which scientific method is *aimed,* and endeavor to define science in terms of its ambition rather than in terms of its accomplishment. We may safely hazard the assumption that the reach of science has as yet exceeded its grasp, that it has tried to do more than it has succeeded in doing.

[7] *Op. cit.,* p. x.

We may accordingly venture on the further assumption that it may do more in the future than it has done in the past, provided of course that we do not take too narrow a view of the future. So it appears that we must judge science not entirely by its method nor by its results but by its aims.

We have been seeking an answer to the question: what does science try to do? Some hint of the answer may be discovered by taking a closer look at scientific method. Scientific method has long been thought to be identical with the logical process of induction, as by Bacon, or, more mystically, identical with intuition, as by Poincaré. Some basis for these identifications occurs in one of the steps of scientific method, which does contain the jump from the sense particulars of common experience to the universal laws which are independent of experience. But surely this is not the whole of scientific method. At both ends of this process of induction, deduction is to be found. For it must be noted that the right inductions or "intuitions" do not occur to just anybody, but only to men who are seeking them, and more especially to men who have had some training in the field. Thomas Hunt Morgan, for instance, a scientist who works exclusively in the field of genetics, is not likely to put forward a brilliant hypothesis belonging in the field of astrophysics. Long and careful study of the previous work in a given science usually precedes scientific discovery. Thus deduction serves as a basis for induction. Again, the generalizations or laws which are reached by induction are tested against the empirical data, and if found to be not invalid, are used as a basis for deductions. Thus scientific laws are, as the American philosopher, Peirce, has pointed out, not merely the summaries of known facts but the finders of new ones. Deduction as well as induction can be a process of discovery.

We have noted, then, that induction is not the whole of scientific method, but that induction is both preceded and followed by deduction. What does this mean? Does it mean that logic and scientific method are one and the same? Not exactly. Scientific method is logic plus the empirical sanction. The abstractive laws of logic, when tested against the run of experience and found to be *not* invalidated, are given the status of scientific laws. We say "not invalidated" advisedly, since the empirical test is a negative one; it contradicts and thus disallows some hypotheses, but cannot prove the validity of any. It tells us when so-called scientific laws are not laws but it does not, and indeed cannot, tell us when they are. Thus there is no known way to place the truth of a scientific law forever beyond doubt. Such is, nevertheless, the intention of science. To discover laws which are as far as possible beyond doubt is the aim of every science, and this goal is one which is approached always more and more closely, even if never reached absolutely. That science whose laws are the least in doubt, and which seems to be approaching the nearest to eternal laws in its formulations, is the best science.

The Nature of Science

We have found out through scientific method something of what science tries to do. It endeavors to abstract from actuality the independent conditions according to which actuality is made possible. That is to say, science endeavors to discover the "laws of nature." This is a definition which, so far, every scientific man would probably be willing to accept. But what does "nature"

mean in this sense? In this last question we have posed
a problem concerning which there is little agreement.
But, proceeding on the basis of the examination we have
just made into method, we are forced to accept Hartmann's definition,[8] and say with him that " 'Nature' is
only an expression for the totality of eternal laws not
made by man." Science, then, tries to discover the
totality of eternal laws not made by man.

Surely we have come a long way from the subjective
definitions of science which we examined at the start
of our inquiry. According to these definitions, science
was first equated with what the scientist thinks, then
more objectively with what he does, and lastly with the
method he follows. These were all rejected. For we
found that science must be defined in terms of what
the scientific method seeks. Science, then, may be defined as a certain means of striving toward the attainment of a certain end. The means is that of empiricism
or scientific method: a series of inductions and deductions, starting from the level of common sense experience, and reaching to ever higher and higher abstractive
levels, while the particulars of sense experience are constantly being sampled in order to make sure that they
are not contradicted by the laws of the higher levels.
The end is that of the discovery of the "totality of
eternal laws." It is this means and this end which make
up what we understand by science.

The history of science reveals a sharply increasing desire on the part of scientists to speculate on the theory
of science. The abstract and philosophical question of
what science is in itself has begun to be a matter of
much concern to the scientists, and the infinite variety

[8] Nicolai Hartmann, Ethics (London, 1932), I, 203.

of their conclusions leads us to the conviction that, regardless of which theory of science proves to be right, most of them must be wrong. There is the danger that the course of science will be led astray by the speculations, no less than by the avowed abrogation of speculation, of the scientists themselves. For this reason, it is well to know, and for the scientist to bear in mind, what the aim of science is. The definition of science as well as of scientific method must be kept constantly before the scientists.

In the beginning of this section, we used our disagreement with the opinions of some scientists as the starting point for discussion. We may close, therefore, by presenting some corroboration among the writings of the scientists for the position here set forth. We have said that the scientists do not agree among themselves in the matter of abstract definition. This is perfectly true. We are, however, able to call to our defense three of the greatest and most respected scientists of the day: Albert Einstein and Max Planck, the physicists, and Alexis Carrel, the biologist.

Einstein is fully cognizant of the fact that science does not depend upon the subject, that the subject who does the investigating merely discovers and does not "create" scientific laws. He says that "the belief in an external world independent of the perceiving subject is the basis of all natural science." [9] This would seem to make the subject matter of science the objective world of phenomena perceived by the subject, the data of sense experience. But not at all. Carrel tells us that this is not the subject matter of science, either.

---

[9] Albert Einstein, *The World as I See It* (New York, 1934), p. 60.

From the things encountered in the material world, whether atoms or stars, rocks or clouds, steel or water, certain qualities, such as weight and spatial dimensions, have been abstracted. These abstractions, and not the concrete facts, are the matter of scientific reasoning. The observation of objects constitutes only a lower form of science, the descriptive form. Descriptive science classifies phenomena. But the unchanging relations between variable quantities—that is, the natural laws, only appear when science becomes more abstract.[10]

But if the subject matter of science is not the subject of knowledge, which Einstein has discarded, nor the object of knowledge, which Carrel has discarded, then what in heaven's name can it be? To this question we are given the same reply by both men. It is the independent laws, which come to the subject through the object of knowledge but remain forever and always independent of the knowledge process. "In a certain sense," says Einstein, "I hold it true that pure thought can grasp reality, as the ancients dreamed." [11] And Carrel formulates the same conception in an even more precise fashion. He proclaims that, "For modern scientists, as for Plato, Ideas are the sole reality." [12] The same conviction is expressed by Max Planck, who understands very well that science is searching for eternal law. "From the fact that in studying the happenings of nature we strive to eliminate the contingent and accidental and to come finally to what is essential and necessary, it is clear that we always look for the basic thing behind the dependent thing, for what is absolute behind what is

[10] Alexis Carrel, Man, the Unknown (New York, 1935), p. 1.
[11] Op. cit., p. 37.
[12] Op. cit., p. 236.

relative, for the reality behind the appearance and for what abides behind what is transitory." [13]

Thus we see in the convictions of three of our leading scientists the affirmation of our own position. These quotations are offered by way of illustration rather than as proof. It is probable that were all scientists equally conscious of their profoundest beliefs they would support the same view. In a religious sense, surely every great scientist must understand that in being a scientist he is serving a cause whose ultimate purpose and fulfillment lies beyond him, that science is in no way a subjective and personal affair but rather an effort toward an end in the course of which the subject is to some extent sacrificed, that, in short, there is a sense in which men exist for science and not science for men. And with the attainment of this understanding, definition can go no further.

Scientific Method

In the effort to account for scientific method, it must be remembered that there has been a classic struggle between the realistic dogmatism of the Church and the nominalistic dogmatism of the radical empiricists among experimental scientists. The Church no longer has any force, but philosophers have inherited the mantle of rationalism. Scientific method is thought to have everything (or nothing) to do with reason. As we shall endeavor to show, however, it consists of the proper blending of logic and experimentation.

The effort at clarification of scientific problems introduces cosmological implications. The confinement of speculation to the minutiae of science is inconsistent

[13] Max Planck, *Where is Science Going?* (London, 1933), p. 198.

with the larger interests at stake. This is a fact which the modern positivists are loath to admit. Earlier philosophers of science have been occupied with the questions raised by empiricism; logical positivists are preoccupied with their own occupation. The advance in the understanding of science on the part of the various positivistic schools, let us say from Mach to Bridgman, has consisted in a gradual reduction to absurdity. At the other extreme, dogmatic idealists in effect dismiss science through superficial sublation by deeming it an intuitionally created contribution to human culture. But despite the fact that the relation of logic to experiment has been effectively derived by such careful scholarship as that of Burtt in his *Metaphysical Foundations of Modern Physical Science* (New York, 1932), and has been sufficiently set forth by such brilliant and original thinkers as Peirce, the two aspects of scientific method still remain in the opinion of most persons mysteriously opposed.

Although science received its start from metaphysics, its nominalism from the mediaeval controversies of Berengar, Roscellinus, Occam, and others, it has seemed to progress by means of a program calling for the active encouragement of applied empiricism and for the strict prohibition against philosophical speculation. Needless to say, philosophy cannot be dismissed this easily, and the adoption of such an attitude is in effect the adoption of a philosophy: namely, that of nominalism. Without wishing to attribute any geographical or chronological location to ideas, it may be pointed out that the British philosophers of the seventeenth and eighteenth centuries concerned themselves with the dilemma of nominalism, brought to the fore through the attempt to find for experimentation some frankly realistic justification which did not seem to be forthcoming. Meanwhile on the continent the older tradition of systematic metaphysics was being maintained without any attention to the new requisite of empiricism, and was no less nominalistic. British empiricism, to which was added the radical empiricism of the Vienna school, and continental rationalism, have come down to us as the alternative positions it is thought possible to assume in the face of the given state of knowledge.

But such a dichotomy is indefensible, as will be made plain by an examination of scientific method itself. The solution of difficulties in scientific method has been the ambition of all modern philosophy, which has, however, vacillated from one extreme view to another without coming to anything acceptable. Scientific method, however, is not difficult to grasp. It consists chiefly of two main steps: (a) From an examination of the conditions of actuality an explanatory hypothesis is inductively formed. The hypothesis is then checked against actuality for allowance or disproof. That is, if the facts of actuality do not disprove the hypothesis (and a single instance can effectively do this) it is assumed to be allowed. Allowance only means not effectively disproved. Proof is never forthcoming, since any future instance of actuality, occurring against enormous probable odds, may constitute a disproof. The checking of hypotheses by the facts of actuality for allowance or disproof is the rôle played by experimentation in scientific method.

After the first step has been successfully accomplished there is yet another to be taken. (b) The hypothesis must be reconciled with the given body of existing knowledge in the science in which it occurs; that is, it must be tested for logical consistency. This step consists in the deduction of the hypothesis from the established principles and laws of the science. If it is found to form with them a unified and self-consistent system, it is assumed to have become worthy of being considered under the status of law. A law is not an eternal truth but an approach to eternal truth, since any scientific law is capable of being subsumed by some more general formulation. It enjoys the truistic state of being eternally valid only to the extent to which it continues to hold true. Nevertheless, the aim of all science is the discovery of the widest and most inclusive laws which are the least altered by the changing context of actuality, and which are thus least susceptible to revision.

It should be evident from the foregoing that experiment and logic, far from being contradictory, are the two necessary parts of scientific method; either one alone cannot justify the appellation of scientific. That this assertion is denied by uncompromising philosophers who see in experimentation only a threat to the authority of reason, as well as by uncompromising empiricists who see in logic only the uncontrolled dogmatizing of the scholastics, does not in any way change the situation. For illustration we have only to point to the illustrious examples set by the great scientists of the past and present. The occasional writings of Copernicus, Galileo, Boyle, Lavoisier, Newton, and Einstein all evince a thorough comprehension of the dual function of scientific method. They have all understood that the laws of logic can never be violated if the results of experimentation are to have any validity, but that, on the other hand, theories of speculation will have to be carefully tested against actuality if they are not themselves to become ridiculously mythological. They have understood that the appeal to actual fact is necessary in the interests of an inquiry into the nature of existence, in order that the most universal principles of that existence should be made known. What happens does so because it is possible, but mere possibility of happening can never become an event. To achieve actuality, possibilities must be twisted and distorted into a spatio-temporal framework within the reach of experience.

The controversy between the defenders of logic and those of experiment can be settled by an appeal to scientific method, which shows both disciplines to be essential parts of an integral process. The epochal systematizers of science have dipped into the conditions of actuality, fully comprehending that they would find there hints and confirmation of conditions that are independent of actuality. The scientific temper does not admit of the distinction between logic and experiment except as parts of a whole. Its greatest exemplars have been neither idle speculators nor laboratory men exclusively, but have deftly employed both occupations as requirements for the advance of true science.

Science and Belief

Experimentation, then, is a way of checking the hypotheses of science. The hypotheses themselves are efforts to arrive at scientific laws which shall be actually valid, non-contradictory with fact as well as consistent with the given body of knowledge in the science. Thus logic is one with experimentation, and rationality lies at the basis of science. So much for the element of rationality in science; but what about actual procedure? Here the question of rationality arises again, but in a somewhat different form. For science cannot actually proceed without scientists to carry it forward, and the existence of such things as scientists is predicated upon a rational acceptance of the whole business of the aims and logico-experimental method of science. In other words, there must be persons who are convinced of the validity and value of science if science as an activity is to be continued. Scientists, then, are among the prerequisites of science.

There is the danger that such a doctrine as we have been expounding in the foregoing paragraph will be interpreted subjectively. The subjective interpretation, however, is always eventually an irrational affair, and is not in any sense the one intended here. The distinction can be properly explained only if a short digression into the nature of belief is allowed. Belief in science being a definite example of belief, we must be pardoned a few words on this topic in general. .

Belief for a long while has been understood to be equivalent to conscious belief. In recent years it has been learned that there are levels below consciousness, the discoveries and general theories of the Freudian psychologists having made us acutely aware of the existence of these levels. The terms "levels" and "below" are used here with some misgivings, since they have such crude visual and spatial connotations. The levels below consciousness are, however, by no means to be comprehended in such a crude sense; we know nothing of their spatial location beyond the fact that they are associated in some way with the human organism. With this in mind then we can proceed to the next necessary caution, namely that we are not speaking in terms of Freudian psychology at all; the Freudian system in our usage is merely analogous and illustrative.

We may explain the situation best by stating and comparing the levels of belief which are matters of ordinary fact. There is (a) the superficial level of mere awareness. Theories and facts may be known about but not accepted. For instance, we may be aware of the existence of Christian Science, or of mental telepathy, without having to believe in them. Here our belief is merely in the existence of the theory. There is (b) the level of conscious belief. At this level, we are aware of the theory and we believe also in its truth. For instance, let us say that we believe in the second law of thermodynamics, which means that we are familiar with the law and we believe that all physical objects are within its range of applicability. There is (c) the level of what we may term, for want of a better phrase, unconscious belief. At this level we believe in a theory or a fact often without even knowing that we hold such a belief. For instance, we may count on immortality without at all knowing that we do so.

The levels of belief, as we have stated them here, are ranged in the order of their strength and importance. The third and last is the most elusive yet it is at the same time the most powerful. Unconscious beliefs are beliefs for which sufficient reasons have been found—and forgotten. They are beliefs which have entered into and affected every phase of our being. Often beliefs go so deep with us that not only we are not aware of them, but may in some cases even go so far as to deny them. Your avowed misanthropist will act from impulse to save a person in danger should the occasion arise. Since action from impulse is not irrational, impulses resting as they do upon deductive levels, it comes about that there is often a sharp contradiction between beliefs as stated and beliefs as implied by actions. The former are conscious; the latter unconscious. By and large, it is what a man does that reveals his "innermost nature," i.e., his unconscious beliefs. It is usually safe to act from impulse only because in most cases our impulses rest upon beliefs which are sounder than those our consciousness is testing, though this is not always so. Beliefs reach unconsciousness only after their truth has been tried in consciousness; hence they tend to be older than conscious beliefs and to have a larger social agreement.

Let us return now to the question of belief in science. Individuals must be convinced beyond reasonable doubt of the value of the purpose and the validity of the method of science before they can become scientists. Since scientific method is rational, this means that no scientist would allow anything to challenge a statement made in his science unless it could prove its authority to do so by means of reason. It would have to be a contradiction in fact (experimentation) or a contradiction in theory (checking against accepted law). Both are wholly rational. Social pressure has no effect in science; the scientist does not accept a new discovery or general theory because other scientists in the same field have done so. He wants in most cases to make the tests himself. This does not amount to an anti-social surrender to individualism; it means simply the recognition of the sole authority of reason. The scientist is a rationalist whose acceptance of the rational nature of the aims and methods of science has penetrated to unconscious levels. Science has, so to speak, become incorporated in his bones to an extent of which he himself is seldom aware. It has become part of the form of his being, and he can sooner change his sex than abandon his belief in science.

The Science of Politics

We have devoted an amount of space to the nature of science and scientific method in the abstract which is perhaps disproportionately large. It has been necessary to do so because the extremely controversial character of these subjects has made it imperative to dissociate certain objectionable theories from the theory which we regard as true, and also because we have wanted to bear well in mind the abstract topic which we hope to apply to politics.

Let us now turn to politics, in order to determine to what extent scientific principles are applicable. The first task in the scientific examination of politics is akin to that which a logical examination would demand: namely, adequate definition. What is the field of politics? It is that division of the social field which concerns the public relations of individuals to some final central authority or authorities. The authority, a government of some sort, is conceded willingly or unwillingly to be decisive in all affairs concerning relations between individuals, between individuals and the state, and between individuals and other states, and between the state and other states. The term "final" is not meant to imply anything absolute, but merely indicates that there is no further individual or social authority to which the aforementioned authority is subordinate. And needless to say, the term "central authority" is here meant to apply to democracies as well as to dictatorships, to kingdoms as well as to communistic states. Authority is centralized qua authority, however it be mediated through representatives or remote agents.

We come, then, to the question of the field of politics as a science. The science of politics would be that science which is concerned with the field of politics as we have defined it. The aim of the science of politics is the discovery of the totality of eternal laws conditioning the public relations of individuals to a final central authority. Social laws when found must prove to be those discovered but not made by man. It is to be admitted that so far no laws of this character are known. We may assume from the fact that all laws exist to be known that some political laws, at least, will in time become a matter of familiarity. Their knowledge must wait upon the discovery of the proper application of scientific method to the political field. It should be admitted at the outset that the social studies, among which we must number politics, are not sciences as yet. The abstract formulation of a subject matter, its investigation by means of a rigorous scientific method, and the result in invariant laws having a tremendous sweep of applicability to peoples at all times and in all places, has not been achieved. All that we can hope to accomplish now, therefore, is to decide which political system conforms the most to the requirements of scientific method, and to compare the operation of that system with the demands of that method.

The laws of a given science tend to become outdated and changed to some extent, and this fact has been responsible for the labeling of scientific laws in some quarters as relative affairs. Scientific conditions, however, are not relative but absolute. Scientific laws are relative because they seldom correspond to the conditions. When they do achieve such correspondence they are absolute. There is indeed in every well-established science a growing central core of absolute law which does not become changed. The relativity of scientific formulations is an outcome of the limitations of human knowledge, which sometimes mistakes hypotheses for laws.

It follows that for every given social condition there must be one and only one proper kind of government. Of two political systems one must be nearer to the relations demanded by the natural conditions than the other; that is to say, one must be nearer the scientific ideal than its rival. The discovery of which is the proper choice in terms of our chosen criterion is not an easy one to render. It is difficult because of the obstacles in the way of the proper application of scientific method. Despite these obstacles, which are those of complexity of subject matter and hence also of ignorance, it is necessary to hazard a few conclusions, always with the understanding that these may be badly in need of revision.

It will be seen at once that democracy is the system of politics which is nearest to the ideal of science. The shortcomings of democracy may be great, but they are not as great as those of other contemporary political choices. Fascism is an irrational affair and hence wholly unscientific. Communism asks us to accept too much in the way of dogmatism; it is too fixed to be a thoroughly scientific choice, though it does hold the possibility of evolving into one. Only democracy remains, for the reasons which we shall set forth. Here a word of caution is necessary. It should be remembered that the political system which we are discussing is ideal democracy, or democracy as it ought to operate. Actual democracy has shortcomings which are due to mistaken or corrupt application, and it is logical, or ideal, democracy which has the capability of being scientific.

Democracy requires the same unconscious belief in its rationality as does science. To question the validity of democracy is to disbelieve in it, for we must not even be aware of our belief if it is to be profound enough to mean anything. Individuals in a democratic polity must be, like scientists, rationally convinced beyond reasonable doubt of the logic of democracy if it is to function scientifically. Legal codification must be available to the endeavors of scientific method; that is to say, all codification must rest upon rational and empirical allowance. For an hypothesis to become accepted as a law, it must be subjected to the strictures of allowance by experience and conformity with the existing body of laws.

Perhaps the essence of scientific democracy would be the susceptibility of all codes to revision.[14] Science can expand its systems no faster than it can verify them. This is the meaning of "Occam's Razor" in the logic of science. There is a further sense in which no scientific statement can be absolutely verified. Thus although there must be some established laws if there is to be any social order, care must be taken to insure the final susceptibility of all codes to revision. Political revolution is always a sign that Occam's caution has been extremely neglected; such a malady is avoidable, if only the scientific attitude of probability toward statements of hypothetical character be taken. In the final analysis,

---

[14] The susceptibility of all codes to revision has in the past been part of the wisdom of canon law, and was suggested by the early founders of the American democracy. But the principle must be carried further in scientific democracy; it has got to be incorporated in the explicit theory of democracy and employed constantly in practice.

all empirical statements are hypothetical. From the fundamental wording of the national Constitution to the most insignificant of municipal traffic ordinances, every law must stand ready equally to be obeyed to the fullest or changed altogether in terms of some better juristic findings. For a scientific democracy would demand at once extreme adherence to laws and the eagerness to exchange them for better laws.

This pair of demands is more easily stated than followed. The average citizen expects modification in terms of extenuating circumstances, where he has tried to follow the law and failed; to say nothing of his efforts at evasion. William James has taught us to get by with whatever we can, since that is the way to the truth of a situation. Extreme adherence to law requires first a strength of character possessed as yet by few persons, and the kind of unconscious belief in the necessity of certain laws which is probably the property as yet of nobody. But if we suppose, for the purpose of illustrating scientific democracy in action, that we did have the necessary strength of character and depth of unconscious belief, could we then imagine in our wildest dreams that these would not to some extent conflict? An unconscious belief is something which almost in its very nature is not easy to dismiss. To believe in laws to the extent to which extreme adherence would demand would also mean to be unwilling to have them replaced by others. Yet just this very combination of circumstances is the prerequisite for the establishment of scientific democracy. And it means that scientific democracy calls for even greater rationality than does physical science. This latter fact should not be surprising in view of the vastly greater complications of the social field.

One more point remains to be considered. We have said that scientific method requires the judicious blending of logic and experimentation. And we have seen that in politics logic demands that state power remain in the possession of the citizens. Now we shall see that experimentation demands that state power in the hands of the citizens must not be allowed to degenerate into mob rule.

Mob rule places leadership exclusively in the hands of the people. By "exclusively" here is meant that there is absolutely nothing beyond themselves to which the people in this sense are answerable, not even the authority of reason. It is a famous observation that mobs do many things which individuals composing the mobs live to regret bitterly in their more rational moments. There are only a few short steps from mob rule to fascist dictatorship. Fascism disciplines the mob as it finds it. If mob rule places leadership exclusively in the hands of the people, fascist dictatorship places leadership exclusively in the hands of wardens. The wardens are usually those who have tended to be the most prominent of the mob.

Democracy as the rule of reason is obliged to avoid the pitfalls of dictatorship and mob rule. The difference is not a new discovery. Jefferson, for example, was thoroughly cognizant of the distinction between democracy and mob rule. There is a middle course between the extremes of no individual and authoritative leadership, exemplified by mob rule, and of one supreme individual having sole authoritative leadership, exemplified by fascist dictatorship. The problem of democracy is one of nicety of adjustment: how much freedom combined with how much authority, assuming that the freedom and the authority must stem from reason and from reason alone.

It is noteworthy that the mob is a feature of Western culture. The primitives do not have unruly mobs, and except in certain rare instances neither do the Eastern societies. What can this mean? The answer stands out in cruel relief. Western culture has not yet been accepted by its adherents with the same degree of finality that other cultures have enjoyed. Our civilization is still superficial; the set of beliefs upon which it is founded are only skin-deep. We have observed how beliefs must be accepted before the actions based on them can appear instinctive. Belief must be incorporated in the bones, must penetrate down below the conscious level, if it is to hold. We are consciously and keenly aware of everything which makes up the foundations of our Western culture. This is an intolerable situation, and one that cannot be maintained for very long. The success of a culture must rest upon its implicit and unwitting acceptance. In this sense the degradation of the democratic doctrine cannot be said to represent a failure. It cannot fail now because it has never been tried, and it has not been properly tried because it has never been accepted in the fullest sense.

Mob rule, the father of its opposite, fascist dictatorship, springs from the unconsidered emotional side of man. No emotion, however, was ever entirely unconsidered. Emotions which have a bad effect rest upon bad reasons long forgotten.[15] Emotions which are, as we say, sound, rest upon reasons equally long forgotten but good. Reasons have to be deeply grounded before conscious feelings spring from them. We have to be unconsciously

[15] Thus extreme rationalism is not rational at all.

convinced of the truth of a thing before we consciously "feel that it is right." Democracy must come to be the instinctive feeling for a considered but forgotten basis.

Dictatorship, perhaps the oldest political solution of all, always has the briefest life. It is too tense and requires the use of too much force, to be able to hold on for very long. Fascism is helplessly dependent upon the existence of a strong external adversary against whom it is necessary to remain on guard. The efforts at the establishment of an international community, eventually demanded by the scientific fact that the natural laws of society can admit of no exception, can be successful only with the surrender to an international authority, which must not be construed as a party, a class, or a people, but as reason. And since the laws of reason are final conditions whether we know it or not, driving us into contradiction and hence actual conflict when we run counter to them, it is the business of scientific politics actually to seek out the conditions of government upon which any lasting government must depend.

Among the forms of government with which we are familiar, democracy is closest to the demands of the method of science. Democratic principles by allowing for adequate revision tacitly admit their tentative nature. No eventual uncertainty is intended but only an experimental attitude: the seeking among relative political formulations not for one that is absolutely relative but for one that is relatively absolute. The balance, in politics as well as in all other fields which are amenable to scientific treatment, is not an easy one to maintain. Reasoning must be corrected by actual experience, and at the same time all practice must be subjected to the control of hypothesis if not of law.

Individual leadership is irrational because too authoritative; mob rule in the form of unguided mass action is irrational because nonrepresentative. The first errs against logic, the second against experience. Hence the task of democracy is to represent scientific method in action by admitting no authority except reason and no collective action which is not considered. The last conclusion is that democracy—as it ought to be—is the nearest that present-day knowledge enables us to come to the practice of scientific method in politics.

8.

The Aims of a Social Life

Logical Outcome of Selfish Feeling

ONE OF THE MOST UNIQUE CHARACTERISTICS OF OUR modern society is the absence of a feeling of responsibility on the part of its individual members. The average citizen is kept constantly aware that he has arrayed against him in the majority of his daily struggles the wilderness of other individuals, with only some pitiful few of whom he exchanges any sympathy; and so he feels that he must get as much as he can while giving as little as possible. Even the leaders, with solitary exceptions, find little need to make social contributions, seeing in their positions open material advantages which it would be forthright foolishness not to take. This is a situation for which the citizen cannot himself be blamed. Our society was originally constructed on the basis of an absolute individualism; it was cast in terms of privilege rather than of obligation. No wonder that it has resulted in the more or less deliberate cultivation of selfishness, with the corresponding neglect of those who could not in every way shift for themselves.

Unfortunately for such a result, however, the latter

class is one to which each of us in some sense belongs. Due to the rapid changes in industrial progress, many through no fault of their own are economically dependent; others who are relatively or altogether free from the relentless strain of getting a living are yet dependent upon professionals for their psychological, moral or religious guidance. The inherited social philosophy of the eighteenth century, on which our modern states are founded, denies the reality of social organization, deeming it to consist merely in the aggregation of self-seeking persons. But the complex interdependence of modern social relations furnishes the contradictions which sweep away the claims of such a theory. If there is such a thing as a "social contract" which has been entered into voluntarily and with conscious knowledge, it must have been drawn in the epoch before men were men.

The chaos which is the modern world is all too familiar to require lengthy description. We take it as axiomatic that we were not born merely to die, and the common theory that life is a striving toward ends must have its outlet in practice, even if this means no more than to go somewhere in a Ford after dinner. The primary urge to "do something" adopts the cross-purposes of myriad programs, and the consequent action resembles nothing so much as the frantic efforts of a colony of ants to escape when their anthill is removed. The little purposes which keep us busy substitute the waste of drift for the bad conscience of idleness, a dubious gain. The friction of our social life is like the heat generated in a gas by the collision of molecules, yet while the loose organization which results from the fact that we cannot go very far without bumping into each other may answer the minimal requirements for holding us together, it can hardly be sufficient ever to bring about social advance.

The helpless dependence of modern man upon thousands of his fellows asserts the reality of society, as does also the whole level of interrelations between societies. That societies act through the agency of members is no more argument against the reality of societies than the fact that human organisms act through the agency of organs is an argument against the reality of human organisms. The reality of organization is a brute fact which must be faced if there is to be either the saving of personal autonomy or the continuation of social progress. Thus in order that society may be of benefit to each and every individual playing a rôle in its composition, some understanding of responsibility to and for that society must be restored to the individual and some feeling of obligation returned him. The accomplishment of this task will put the world back on the path toward the recovery of the ideals which it has momentarily lost, and this in turn will have the effect of substituting for random action a directed activity.

The question may well be asked: How is this to be done? How indeed is the individual, trained in selfishness even past his own cognizance, to be made aware of the fact that his welfare is not a limited thing which can be narrowly pursued, and that in order to seek his own prospering, he must be deeply concerned with the welfare of society? The task is certainly difficult, and its obstacles at first glance appear insurmountable. Often, however, it is possible to triumph because of difficulties rather than in spite of them. In the facing of any problem, we must take actual conditions for granted, and endeavor to build upon them. Perhaps in order to reawaken the social conscience of the selfish individual, that selfishness itself must be employed.

Let us begin our inquiry, then, by assuming that social feeling can be founded upon selfishness. This leads us immediately to an examination of what is meant by the self. For just what is the self; does it consist in the somatic organism? But the body is able to undergo severe changes without loss of the self; and, on the other hand, in cases of dual personality, one self seems to supplant another without any discoverable corresponding somatic change. Moreover, the body can continue when the self is lost; those who are violently insane manifest no knowledge of self. The only identity which appears to persist throughout the violent shifts between the somatic organism and the self is the fact of awareness. Is the self, then, the act of awareness? But this cannot be, either, since the identity of the self is sometimes maintained in the absence of consciousness, as in states of coma and deep sleep. Lastly, it may be asked whether the self is the soul. But this is an hypothetical entity for which no equivalent has been found at any level of investigation. If nothing mystical is meant by the soul but merely Aristotle's psyche or organization of the organism, we are nearer the answer to our question, but soul in its modern sense is too vague to denote anything.

The last suggestion has approached close to the correct answer to our inquiry. We have been looking for something which the self could be, but the self is not a "thing" at all. That is to say, it is not a thing as thing is conceived by substance-minded thinkers. Still, neither is it nothing. By the term "self" should be understood a locus for the assemblage of qualities and relations. Thus the self is truly not a thing but an historical identity which is known through its relations with things, a receptacle for qualities in relation. In this sense a stone just as much as a man may be said to have a self. But the higher we rise in the organizational series of identities, the more qualities and relations the self enjoys. Thus a man has vastly more than a stone, and it is with the former that we are concerned in this work. Yet in order to clarify the viewpoint here maintained, the similarity should be borne in mind.

At the social level, this explanation of the self is easily exemplified. For there is no such thing as an utterly isolated person. No one can be said to be complete who has not a family and friends. The individual can be understood only as a member of society, having interdependent relations with a widening circle of its other members, relations which are seen to be less and less limited. Each and every individual is what he is, not exclusively through his own endeavors, but also by virtue of his remotely regressive inheritance and his infinitely extended environment. Thus a man is not an independent creation, for which either himself or an exclusively transcendent deity may be given sole credit, but rather he is the universe straining after a man.

At the economic level, social interdependence is obvious. What American, for instance, can be said to be economically independent of other Americans? The automobile worker is involved in the success of the motion picture industry, and the latter in the profitable crops of the cotton planter, and so on. And is not the American dependent upon the Irish for his linen, the Liberians for his rubber, the Chileans for his copper, the Japanese for his silk? Through a complicated set of ramifications, which embraces us all and yet is peculiar for each individual, everyone is finally involved with everyone else. Thus economic dependence requires the whole of society. But the dependence of the individual certainly does not end with society. The continuance of mere physical existence reaches out beyond social economics to the remotest confines of the physical world. For human existence is momentarily dependent on rivers to remain where they are, on the geologic earth to stay at its present consistency, on the air not to change its proportions, on solar radiation to continue at its present rate, and so forth, until dependence finally embraces the whole universe of being.

It is true, of course, that the more intricate, extended and interdependent such relations are, the more unstable they prove. The host of conditions necessary to their existence is hard to maintain intact. This is as evident in social organization as in any other kind. Moreover, the disruption of such interdependent relations on any grand scale is always disastrous for the individual. The vast interlockings of social relations are insistent in their collapse; they do not grow apparent until they have ceased to be effective, just as certain internal organs of the body only make themselves felt through pain. Social revolutions have the immediate effect of confusing everything for the individual, and of causing his world to appear to have resolved itself into utter chaos. The downfall of the old social organizations and the effort to set up new ones represent to the average individual only a time of troubles, a period when the sudden understanding of his own predicament, and the imminent demands made upon him for judgments of a far-reaching nature, seem too much for his meagre abilities. It is then that, in the words of Élie Faure, he longs for the policeman or for death. Once the old state of affairs is gone, any substitute appeals to him to be a better one than trying to live through an interim period without any order, even in an effort to discover and establish the best possible one. He wishes with all his heart that he could retreat into any limited order which will give him something certain upon which he can lean. For it is a feeling of safety that he comes to desire most of all, and not to be forced to adventure into unknown regions of possibilities whose apparently infinite variety is appalling.

But this urge to retrench loyalties, to identify individual interests with as narrow a community as possible, is finally a matter of ignorance, and amounts to the practice of a false economy. The effort to allay the feelings of insecurity, through the discovery of a limited order with its finite goal, is wholly understandable but none the less ill-advised. We may sympathize with it; but we cannot fairly endorse it. For the logic of events is set against any kind of temporary security gained by undependable means. In an important essay, entitled "The Doctrine of Chances"[1] Peirce has shown that to identify one's interests with anything limited is to have acted illogically in the end. Everything actual eventually perishes: other individuals, corporations, states, and even in time the physical universe as predicted by the law of entropy. Thus any actual and hence limited community must prove too narrow and short-lived to justify the loyalty bestowed upon it. If it is true that the self is a set of relations with everything else, then it becomes plain that to be logical about interests is to

[1] Reprinted in Chance, Love and Logic (London, 1923).

identify one's interests with an unlimited community of interests—with the welfare of the entire universe.[2]

The caution is highly important that what is being propounded here is not a doctrine of otherworldliness. The most immediate conclusion following the discovery of the perishability of all finite things is that the actual world does not count in any way whatsoever, and is unworthy of our efforts in its behalf. We should therefore, this argument runs, ignore actuality altogether and concentrate instead upon a reification of the infinite unity of the universe, in the form of some anthropomorphic or abstract deity. But this is an erroneous and fatal conclusion, and not at all necessary. The individual is an actual fact, and he lives and struggles in a sensible and actual world, which is the only theatre of action open to him. Further, this actual world is real, as real (if not as perfect) as anything he can ever hope to experience; and to deny it altogether is to deny participation in a certain part of reality in favor of a nebulous and probably non-existent world of shadowy perfections.

Not to deny this actual world, but to make it more perfect, is the human task. The doctrine of the unlimited community does not present an other world in which the actual and sensible things of this world exist in all their shining perfection. It recognizes that beyond the limited communities which are actual lie the possibility of wider and still wider communities, in an indefinite series of inclusiveness. And it calls upon the individual to work toward the most unlimited community through the limited communities at hand. Limited communities are to be accepted and utilized but

[2] For the expansion of this notion as the true rational ethics for democracy, see Chapter XIII.

not considered as final ends; they are to be employed instead as stepping stones to wider and wider communities. Thus although the individual is to strive always toward an unlimited community in a quest which is perhaps by its very nature doomed to final failure, the case is not as black as it might at first glance seem. For even if the most unlimited community cannot be attained, by using limited communities as means instead of accepting them as ends the individual is sure to gain access to less and less limited communities, and thus to have contributed something in his own age toward the social progress of humanity.

Selfishness, then, understood on the broad and not on the narrow view, turns out to be an affair of enlightened self-interest. The program does sound something like a demand for self-sacrifice; but self-sacrifice is the most intelligent kind of self-interest, provided only that what the individual sacrifices himself for is the widest of social goals. If every person were to recognize the truth of this logic, the amount of actual self-sacrifice required would be minimal for each individual, while, on the other hand, the total amount of benefits accruing would be very great. Enlightened self-interest is interest which goes outward to all beings. The saint is one who instinctively recognizes the validity of this position. He wishes to own nothing, and asks for no receipt for services rendered. Such services are their own source of satisfaction, because all of the elements in the multiplicity of the saint's relations with everything else are equally the grounds for his intense enjoyment. The saint may be rightly described as the most intelligently selfish of men.

Peirce, Freud and Adler

It will be illustrative here to compare Peirce's theory with the corresponding social implications of Freudian and Adlerian psychology. To some extent at least, the social implications of psychoanalysis are implicit rather than explicit, but they are all the more subtly effective for that, especially in therapeutic practice. The Freudian psychology takes for granted the inherently evil and anti-social nature of the individual, who is controlled in his evil impulses only by his own conscience (called the "super-ego") and by the "censor" which operates in terms of the accepted customs and institutions of a limited society. The aim of psychoanalytic therapy is the adjustment of the unfortunate individual to the demands ordinarily put upon him by this limited and actual community in which he is obliged to function. Thus the immediate social environment of any neurotic is taken as the norm to which with the help of psychiatry he must become adjusted, or remain neurotic.

At this point the Freudian application is confronted with a difficulty, in terms of the broader social life which it is supposed to serve. For obviously there are two kinds of maladjusted individuals. There are those who fail to meet the demands of a social life, either because of a physiological defect (psychosis), or because they are inhibited through some accidental failure in their past which they have forgotten or to which they attach little if any importance (neurosis). But there are also those who deliberately fail to meet the demands of a social life because they find themselves dissatisfied with the contradictions and disvalues of the limited and actual

society in which they live. To help members of the first
group to become better adjusted to their immediate
social environment would probably be a good accomplishment; but to achieve a like success with the second
group would be in effect to head off the vanguard of
social reform. The intelligent psychoanalyst may be able
to distinguish in most cases; but the important point to
note is that, from the dictates of psychoanalytic theory,
both groups stand in the same relation to the limited
societies which Freudian psychology accepts as the proper
norm.

With Adlerian psychology the situation is somewhat
different. On its theoretical side, the psychology of Adler
and his school may be best described not as psychology
but rather as ethics. Like the Freudians, the Adlerians
wish to adjust the unfortunate individual to society, but
the two schools of psychology differ in their choice of
the societies to which the individual is to be adjusted.
The Freudians, as we have seen, choose the limited and
actual society which forms the individual's immediate
environment, but the Adlerians understand that to adjust
the individual to such a society may often be a dis-
service to the individual and even constitute a social
retrogression. In place of this narrow conception, Adler
constantly speaks of what he calls the "ideal society," a
conception which can easily be reconciled with Peirce's
notion of the unlimited community; Freud's conception,
however, cannot. Adler reverses Freud's social doctrine:
for Freud's evil man in a limited but good society, Adler
substitutes the good man in a limited and therefore
to some extent evil society. The picture presented in
Adler's individual psychology is of men possessed of
inherently right and good impulses, thwarted only by

the limitations of limited societies. In order to effect the therapeutic treatment of the neurotic, says Adler, we must adjust him to the ideal society (i.e., set him the goal of the unlimited community). He will then find himself with a purpose which can avail itself of, instead of being defeated by, any limited and actual society in which he is situated.

To become adjusted to the narrow patterns and petty ambitions of any limited community is truly to be rendered of little worth for the needs of a major social advance. To be unserviceable is to be an unhappy individual. But to become adjusted to an unlimited community is to be disequilibrated with any limited community in a manner which will aid in the overcoming of that limited community's limitations. There is a large and very important distinction to be drawn between the temporary satisfactions of a narrow social adjustment and the wide love of an infinite society. This distinction is to be found between the restrained criminals (which Freud seems to think we are) and the potential social reformers (which Adler gives us credit for being). And it is this same distinction which existed earlier between the work of Hobbes and Machiavelli on the one hand and that of Green and Peirce on the other.

A word of caution is necessary concerning the philosophical status of what Peirce calls the unlimited community and Adler the ideal society. The naive assumption that all possible social goals, which are not yet established but which are posited in order to give actual social progress a direction and an aim, exist only in the thoughts or brains of those who conceive them, will not stand examination. This error follows from the deeper erroneous presupposition that whatever is not physical must therefore be mental. But the actual is not entirely physical, since other things besides the purely physical are actual. President Roosevelt's plan for the reform of the Supreme Court was not physical but was certainly actual; and so is the beauty of *this* sunset, the good deed of *that* person. Moreover, there is nothing which is exclusively mental; what we call mental is merely the mental apprehension of things which are not mental but objective and independent of the mind. Thus conceptions of ideals enjoy a corresponding existence in objective possibility. The future is not yet actual nor wholly physical, yet it is not nothing. And it is emphatically not exhausted by the minds of those who dream and hope, and work toward the actualization of their dreams.

The doctrine of the unlimited community substitutes a rational social goal for an irrational individual one. Our inherited notion of the state as a sort of necessary evil, a self-appointed guardian whose coercive effect must be held to a minimum, is contradictory and irrational, since it denies the valid status of law and order and retreats upon the sole reality of the particular individual. This irrational social philosophy was a good methodological instrument with which to overthrow the empirically unjustified burden of religious strictures in the Middle Ages, but it will not do as a positive philosophy to guide the conduct of modern society. Nor do we have to have it, except as an occasional caution against the unjustifiable erection of superfluous laws. There is no reason why law and social order always have to run wild with their prohibitions against individual freedom of action. The correct sort of rational social order is one whose chief duty would be to discover the exact scientific method in social affairs, through it to further the search for true laws, and then to ensure that they could be followed. Irrelevant interim social matters would meanwhile need to be governed according to the criterion of a farsighted utility and by the dictates of reason.

Democracy and the Social Goal

Liberalism under the radical individualism of negative democracy has been a weapon to be turned against the law, but liberalism under positive rational and social democracy should be freedom to find the law and to follow it. The notion of freedom and the notion of law are by no means opposed, except under irrational political philosophies. The distinction between laws which coerce and laws which allow will make this clear. A coercive law is a bad law, since it sets no one free; to rule against smoking on Thursdays, for instance, would be a bad law because it would permit nothing. But there are other laws which bestow freedom; parking regulations, for instance, enable many to park cars where but few could park otherwise. Again, traffic lights enable everyone to proceed with the utmost dispatch and are intended to prevent nothing but accidents. Absolute freedom in this sense is of course an impossibility, and not even one absolute law applicable to social actuality has as yet been discovered.

But the tendency of all social studies is to utilize all available freedom in an effort to find laws as nearly absolute as possible. The goal, remote though it may be, is none the less the one which dictates all programs for the discovery of the ideal social order. We can imagine that its attainment would illustrate better than anything else the unity of freedom and law, for then absolute freedom and absolute law would establish one and the same set of conditions: socially, a state in which everyone would have to do exactly what he wanted to do.

An ancient adage has thus been reaffirmed in its modern dress, that only the truth can set men free. The family relation between truth and practicality was interpreted in various ways by the pragmatists. Peirce held that the reality of truth necessitates the validity of the practices following from it, but James so far misunderstood Peirce as to reverse this doctrine and make practicality the test of truth. But practicality is suggestive rather than demonstrative of truth, an infinite run of actuality being necessary for the conclusive demonstration by practice of any truth. Truth is practical not because workability determines truth but because the truth always works. Thus although practice may offer hints to the search for truth, another criterion must be introduced into its verification. This criterion is the logical one of self-consistency with already established systems. The attempt to combine these two guides to truth has yielded the discipline termed scientific method. Science is the name given to freedom to find the laws through practical suggestions, theoretical hypotheses, and empirical and logical demonstrations.

In the development of the separate sciences, the physical sciences have been the only ones to meet with any success in the pursuance of the scientific method. With certain narrow reservations it may be asserted that the social sciences have hardly even got started as sciences, a fact which is employed in some arguments to show that scientific method is not applicable at all in social science. But scientific method is not the property of any one science or group of sciences, and the day will come when the social sciences will follow the physical sciences in their successful technique of discovering broader and more inclusive laws. Against those who would erect a failure into a principle, and deny the possibility of an exact social science because there has not yet been any, it can be maintained that the history of positivism is plentifully strewn with arguments to show that certain things which by their very nature could not be done were shortly afterwards accomplished. All such arguments against the attainment of an untried end usually rest on the unfounded assumption that all avenues to its approach are known and have been exhausted. Although there is as yet no social science, we must at least allow for its desirability and pursue its discovery, on the hypothesis that such a science is at least possible.

It must be plain to all that the success of social science is remote, and the objective goal of ethics is meanwhile set as the service of an unlimited community. The mediate approximation of this goal has been shown to consist in the serving of only those limited communities which most nearly approach the unlimited, indeed in working ever toward the unlimited through the least limited. So much for an objective social ethics; but what about the neglected subjective aspects of the problem? Human beings are, after all, individuals, and insist on comprehending their social status after some individual fashion. Marxism, for instance, offers one alternative of the objective social goal in ethical terms, but it provides nothing for the inward individual. Again, the classic approach of introspective psychology has been discredited, rightly enough, because it considers the subject as a self-sufficient organism, containing everything except irrelevant stimuli, and ignores the object. For the purposes of introspection, the psychological subject is a sensitivity-reactivity system in which everything but the reactivity must be elided. The social crisis of our day receives no reckoning from the application of such a conception, even though the individual is primarily a social animal dedicated to the service of the organization which he shares with his fellows. Thus the gap continues to go unfilled, with, on the one hand, a social system failing to account for the subjective aspect of ethics, and on the other, a subjective psychology making no mention of the social aspect of the individual.

The problem to which neither of these studies has succeeded in finding an adequate solution is to explain the subjective ethics of the individual in terms which will adequately describe its real objective properties. Research into the inherently reactive nature of these properties reveals that the idea of character is one which ought to contain the solution in question. It will be immediately observed that character is hardly a new idea in the world; that indeed under one or another of its numerous definitions it has never gone entirely out of prominence. This contention must be admitted to be just. And yet a careful review of the current definitions of character will make evident their insufficiencies. Character for Catholic theology, for instance, has to do with the way in which the holy sacraments mark the soul for the worship of God. But since this God has become vague through romantic mysticism and so lost precision, the character associated with his worship is deemed no longer sufficient for the exigencies of the daily human struggle. Character for the irrationalism of modern individualism will do no better, since there it becomes the aggregate of distinctive moral and mental qualities by which the particular individual is distinguished from others of his kind. But this latter is a definition which denies any connection between the individual and the extra-human world in which he moves, and there is nothing objective about it.

To these definitions of character, positive rational democracy offers a third alternative, which attempts to give a place to the subject's private nature in a public world. Character, on this view, is in the individual the dominant function of austere steadfastness when confronted with obstacles in the pursuit of a goal deemed worthy. That this goal is a social goal need hardly be added. By this definition, the polarity of the individual and society is once more rightly established, but this time without theological autocracy. Individual character is required for the pursuit of the unlimited community. The necessity of holding this balance is most plainly marked by divergencies from it. The psychiatrist is called in when the balance is upset—too much responsibility leads to neurosis; but on the other hand, increasing insanity is also due to the complete lack of a social goal. Between these defections, the individual will be unflinching in his service of society, for he knows failure would only mean that his character and his comprehension of the objective goal were not shared by a sufficient number of his fellows. Apart from complete participation by each and every individual in the common social enterprise, Milton was correct in his assertion that they also serve who only stand and wait.

The day when society can be carried forward by sheer genius alone, if indeed it ever existed, is coming to an end. History recalls endless instances of the single individual with his extraordinary abilities being set over against the masses harboring a cultural lag. To some extent, of course, this situation will probably always remain, but it can be abated. T. H. Huxley once remarked that the advantage of science is that mediocre minds are able to advance it. We have always been in the habit of watching the solitary genius with amazement and stupefaction; now we can help him, and we owe this new social situation to science. But what is true to a large degree of science is already true, even before the development of a valid social science, of the social order. A good general social order would be one which could enable mediocre men to make their small contributions. Final causes are served by innumerable efficients before we are even aware of what is happening, for the simple reason that the *value* of iteration has nothing iterative about it.

It is now apparent that we have returned to our original argument. The value of small contributions is dependent upon the extent to which the mainspring of all action can be maintained in unobscured view. It means, finally, adjustment not to any limited social order but rather to the ideal social order. And adjustment to the ideal social order mediately involves the de *facto* adjustment to the broadest and most perfect of actual social orders. It further involves the attempt to remold the accepted actual social order into something nearer the ideal. The aims of a social life are inherent in the goal of the unlimited community, and are served by the individual's recognition of it in his labors toward its achievement.

We are now in a position to comprehend the part which religion ought to play in the proper social life. By religion here is not meant any of the older varieties of established, orthodox religion. The accepted religions, which wish to confine man's love of deity to his emotional adoration of God without mediation, and his service of deity to the living of a conservative life outside the jurisdiction of the priests, overlook the rational approach, which is by means of mediation forever, through the service of ever larger and more inclusive communities. The past tendency has been to confuse religion with society, based on direct relations between men and God, without the mediation of nature; and this has been a persistent factor in the apparent conflict between science and religion. Society contains religious elements for the individual, but this is very different from saying that society is to be identified for the individual with any orthodox religion.

If we dare speak of individual salvation and social progress in the same sentence, and we certainly can if they are the same ambition treated at different levels of organization, then it becomes evident that the individual can be "saved" only through feeling and that society can "progress" only through reasoning. We must retain in our programs the explicit distinction between adoration at altars and deduction in laboratories. God must still be distinguished from science, not only in the way we catalogue our various activities but, more significantly, in the way we serve. The two services are by no means at odds. We are always free to adore God which is the infinite value of the whole universe, but we must strive upward slowly by collecting the value-accretions of a science which is always itself value-free. The emotional regard of the individual for God can be reconciled with his rational participation in the collective efforts of society to devise a better actual social order. The first is emotional religion, the latter rational science; but the unlimited community toward which they both direct their aspirations is one and the same.

9.

An Analysis of Liberalism

Fallacies of Irrational Individualistic Liberalism

LIBERALISM HAS OCCURRED AS AN ACTUAL PROGRAM ONLY in a brief flicker between the reign of absolutisms. In our day, it occurs in the comparatively short interval between faith in the revealed truths of Christianity and possible faith in the dogmas of communism. By these two absolutisms, liberalism is considered a condemned error. It is specifically condemned by Catholic Christianity. It is specifically condemned by communism. But what is liberalism? Should it be defended or annihilated? In order to determine the answers to these questions it will be necessary first to make an analysis of liberalism. This analysis will reveal that liberalism has been conceived irrationally and is therefore contradictory and fallacious, but that a rational form of liberalism is possible and necessary.

Liberalism may be defined as the freedom of individual thought and action. According to the doctrine of liberalism, the individual is to be left free to think whatever he wishes to think, and to do whatever he chooses to do. Two observations must be made immediately. The first is that freedom of *thought* is something of which no individual can be deprived, inasmuch as thought is a private affair and must therefore remain free. It is seldom possible to tell what a person is thinking about, and more difficult still to dictate the psychological order of his reasoning. Therefore freedom of thought need not be argued here. It is rather with the freedom to express thoughts that the doctrine of liberalism is concerned. The second observation is that *complete* freedom of action is a contradiction. If one wishes to murder a neighbor while he wishes still to live, freedom of action is obviously not possible for both persons. Freedom of individual action, then, must always assume a residual basis of social law which is held to a minimum but operative wherever there is a possibility of conflict between individual courses of action.

Liberalism as defined above, and as historically formulated by the English utilitarian school of Bentham and the Mills, is irrational. It rests upon the theory that only atomic individual particulars are real and that society is but a fictional convention to represent the collection in free association of real atomic individuals. In order to expose the contradictions contained in this irrational individualistic liberalism, it will be necessary to break it down into its constituent assumptions. These are: (1) that the individual's own capacity for reasoning constitutes his final court of appeal; (2) that there is no other guide to individual thought and action except conscious experience; (3) that there exist no universal laws superior to the individual; (4) that consequently no social organization is superior to the individual; and finally, (5) that since there is no certain knowledge possible, individual opinion must always govern. Let us consider each of these assumptions separately.

(1) To maintain that the individual's own capacity for reasoning constitutes his final court of appeal seems to be an affirmation of the authority of reason, but is actually just the reverse. The thesis of the absolutism of individual reasoning is based upon confusion of reason with reasoning. The individual's reasoning refers to an independent reason (i.e., an independent logical order of existence), else it could not be. To consider the reasoning of the individual final is to make the errors of reasoning into something ultimate, since without an independent referent, there would be no way in which errors in reasoning could be detected. But that errors in reasoning are, in fact, detected, is evidence of the existence of an independent reason, an independent truth in terms of which error can be judged.

The final appeal to individual reasoning rests upon a failure to make the necessary distinction between the logical independence of ideas and the psychological process of reasoning. Thinking, which is a psychological process, must not be confused with thoughts, which are the apprehension of ideas by the mind. It is indeed the mind which apprehends ideas, but independent ideas are what the mind apprehends. Thus independent reason or logic, and not individual reasoning, must be the final court of appeal. True rationality rests upon the awareness of an independent reason, and upon the recognition of both success and failure in the individual's attempt to apprehend the conditions of reason through the process of reasoning.

(2) The second assumption of individualistic liberalism is that there is no guide to individual thought and action other than conscious experience. The doctrine of the sole reality of conscious experience as the indi-

vidual's guide is only another way of stating the philosophy of radical empiricism or positivism. We may sum up one objection to it here by asserting that it does not allow any reality to the actual world, and hence gives no objective basis for the judgment of the individual upon his conscious experience. Hence the doctrine eventually reduces to a solipsism which cannot be proved or refuted but which few persons have ever sincerely held.

The appeal to individual conscious experience was made by Descartes, who saw that to prepare the ground for such an appeal it was necessary to start with doubt. He attempted to begin by doubting all but his own existence. But what Peirce has pointed out in this connection remains true, that "no one who follows the Cartesian method will ever be satisfied until he has formally recovered all those beliefs which in form he has given up." [1] We cannot doubt simply because we choose to do so. Doubt is possible only when we have been given sufficient reason. "Let us not pretend to doubt in philosophy what we do not doubt in our hearts," says Peirce.[2] But if we are not able to start with universal doubt, our beliefs cannot be guided wholly by conscious experience.

Yet neither can we start with universal belief. The fact is that we are no more free to believe than we are free to doubt, both demanding logical justification. If belief without sufficient reason were possible, there would be no more basis for accepting one belief than for accepting another. Consequently the beliefs of the individual would be in a constant state of flux, and his mind

[1] Collected Papers, 5.265.
[2] Ibid.

would be a confusion of beliefs many of which would be contradictory, accepted or rejected only according to the current of whim or caprice. But this is a description of insanity. Indeed our sanity does depend upon the fact that we do not accept or reject beliefs without reason. We are free to believe only what we have reason to believe, which is to say that we are not free to believe except what reason allows.

So much for conscious experience as a guide to individual thought. But the same is true when conscious experience is offered as a guide to individual action. Freedom of belief and freedom of action are in fact inseparable doctrines, since actions usually follow from beliefs and each person acts according to what he believes. The failure of belief leads to the failure of action, and contradictory beliefs lead to contradictory actions. Ideas are apprehended intrinsically as feeling, logically as thought, and expressed objectively as action. They do not in any wise have to be conscious in order to exist and to have their effect. We are not free to do whatever we choose to do—at least not when our actions lead to contradictions. The truth shall prevail in the world of actuality simply because contradictions eventually prove themselves obstacles which cannot be overcome. Thus the same conclusion holds for action as for thought: namely, that we are free to do only what we have good reasons to do, which is to say that we are free to do only what an independent logic allows.

(3) The contention that no universal laws exist to govern the individual is refuted by the truth of the laws of logic. Certainly the individual is not free to believe in ultimate contradictions. Moreover, the whole body of scientific and mathematical knowledge can be offered

in refutation. No individual is free to believe, for instance, in any but a one-way process for the radioactive disintegration series of chemical elements. Certainly the individual is governed as to his belief. The contention that no universal laws exist to govern the individual's actions is likewise impossible to maintain. If the individual were always free to act, there would be no need for consistency in our actions, and no searching for rational plans. What we would do would be—whatever we did. But since here, too, sanity is challenged, universal laws must be admitted to exist.

(4) Irrationalism prohibits the allowance of real social organizations superior to the individual. For this philosophy admits the reality of individuals, who, after all, do exist on the physical level as well as other levels, but denies the equal reality of the relations between individuals. If social organization did not govern individuals, men could not exist in a state of society. The division of labor, which makes society possible, and which exists even in primitive societies, depends upon the subordination of the individual to social plans. The old nominalistic explanation of social organization as a mere summatory convenience does not account for the *necessity* of social organization where men are living in collections. From the social point of view, complete freedom of individual action must lead to inevitable contradictions. The chaos resulting from the lack of authority on the part of social organization would allow the contradictions to inhibit all individual action. Thus the fact of the reality of social organization is attested by the mere presence of individuals in the condition of society.

(5) It is doubtful whether anyone sincerely believes

that no knowledge is possible and that opinion alone governs, yet this is an assumption of the appeal to individual reasoning as the sole authority. Science exists for the purpose of transferring ideas from the status of hypothesis to the status of law, from the realm of opinion to that of knowledge. When an hypothesis is suggested in science, reason to doubt it as well as to accept it may exist. No hypothesis is accepted as law without sufficient empirical allowance, plus the proof by self-consistency within the given system; but once such demonstration has been forthcoming, the agreement with regard to it is almost unanimous. If, then, later experimentation provides sufficient evidence to doubt the law, it is discarded, or subsumed by a more general law. This ideal of science is most closely approached by the science of physics. To insist upon the impossibility of knowledge and the primacy of opinion would be to challenge the validity of scientific method. Since, as has been shown in a previous chapter, the method of reason is supported by the method of science, the claim of invalidity for scientific method would be unreasonable. Therefore in so far as science is admitted, knowledge is also admitted to be possible, and opinion admitted to exist only in order to become knowledge.

Subjectivism is irrefutable, yet untenable. The adherence to opinion and the denial of objective knowledge amounts to the adoption of the subjectivist position. To deny that there are any "irreducible and stubborn facts" which resist the individual's desires, and to assert that the world, including all other persons, has been created by the individual's mind, is a position which is safe from logical refutation while remaining inadmissable to enlightened common sense.

We have examined liberalism in its traditional formulation sufficiently to conclude that, as such, it is untenable. Liberalism stated entirely from the point of view of the atomic individual is irrational through and through, and therefore completely invalid. Thus we must turn next to the question of whether a rational social liberalism is possible.

Possibilities of Rational Social Liberalism

Can there be a rational social liberalism? Nineteenth century liberalism, as an explicit affair, was the doctrine formulated by Locke, Bentham, and the Mills, and thus extremely irrational and individualistic. It has frequently seemed necessary to those who have wished to challenge reigning laws, customs and institutions because of demonstrable limitations, first to indicate their subjective nature. Social reformers find it necessary to remind themselves that such laws are man-made in order to feel quite sure that, despite their age and authority, they can be man-destroyed. Yet they always wish to establish the objective validity of the laws they offer in place of the old. The complete denial of the validity of law is hardly the way in which to question prevailing laws. It is necessary only to recognize that all laws are equally independent but not all equally limited. When less limited laws are being substituted for more limited laws, the question of the independence of law should not be involved.

When humanitarian social legislation appeared in the nineteenth century, it did not come as the result of the old irrational individualistic liberalism. Indeed how could it, since the traditional liberalism had set its face against such legalism? But as John Dewey points out, in that century there were already the beginnings of a rational social liberalism evident in social legislation, not due to the accepted version of liberalism. He says that

Benthamite liberalism was not the source of factory laws, laws for the protection of children and women, prevention of their labor in mines, workmen's compensation acts, employers' liability laws, reduction of hours of labor, the dole, and a labor code. All of these measures went contrary to the idea of liberty of contract fostered by *laissez faire* liberalism. . . . Gradually a change came over the spirit and meaning of liberalism. It came surely to be associated with the use of governmental action for aid to those at economic disadvantage and for alleviation of their conditions.[3]

Such is the change from individualistic to social liberalism, as it took place historically, forced by the logic of economic events. Explicitly, the new understanding of liberalism was formulated and vigorously defended by Thomas Hill Green and his followers. Green was an objective idealist, which is to say, something of a rationalist, and he opposed the old liberalism on ethical grounds. The good, he asserted, is not something subjective and individual, but something absolute, and thus the individual is helped in its attainment by and through the perfection of society. As John Dewey says, Green "asserted that *relations* constitute the reality of nature, of mind and of society." [4]

But if relations are real, then laws are real, which means that not only must the perfection of society be the true concern of the individual but also that the authority of social laws must be recognized. But such

[3] John Dewey, *Liberalism and Social Action* (New York, 1935), pp. 20–21.
[4] *Ibid.*, p. 24.

recognition lays an injunction upon belief. Is freedom of thought, then, inconsistent with this conception? Definitely not. On all questions where knowledge cannot be segregated from opinion, liberalism must prevail. In short, *freedom of thought is required more for hypothesis than for law.* In so far as the true relations or laws of existence are discovered, their questioning would be idle and unreasonable. If an hypothesis is put forward as a suggested explanation of anything, its proof or disproof must wait upon evidence; and until such evidence is forthcoming, it can neither be believed as law nor doubted as error. Until reason to believe or doubt is forthcoming, it must occupy an interim realm. It is only toward such hypotheses, toward opinion, then, that the attitude of liberalism is possible.

An important exception must at once be made here. From the formulation of rational social liberalism which we have just been presenting it would seem as though laws once discovered could never again be doubted. This is not true, and rests upon a misunderstanding of the realistic liberal doctrine. The liberal attitude is absolutely excluded only from absolutely ideal laws. The absolute, ideal and logical conditions of existence cannot be questioned; they are just as they are and as they must be. The laws which are discovered by human beings in their search for truth, are approximations of the ideal law. When a science abandons, or rather subordinates, one law to another more general, it is in process of approximating always closer and closer to this ideal law. And in so far (but only in so far) as discovered laws approximate to the ideal, liberalism is compelled to fall away.

When all the sciences reach the same degree of success that has been obtained in physics, the ultimate rule of reason over belief will become apparent, and there will no longer be any claim made for complete freedom of individual opinion. Once the social sciences are in a position to state some of the laws of social conduct, the reason for actions will be apparent, and the conflict of actions arising from conflict of individual opinion will be greatly diminished. Thus the ideal of society (approachable, albeit remote) involves the complete abolition of freedom of thought and its replacement by adequate reason for thought. Inasmuch, however, as such a state of affairs is incredibly remote, a residual rational liberalism is essential to any progress toward it. The proper mode of the attainment of this ideal lies in scientific method. One measure of the success of science in this regard is the ground remaining for freedom of thought within a given subject matter. For example, freedom of thought on questions involving physics is already difficult for the non-professional; whereas such freedom of thought on questions involving politics or any other division of social science is the common and often jealously guarded prerogative of the man in the street. Liberalism must remain, however, and be required for hypotheses, for any state of affairs short of the complete establishment of law.

Rational social liberalism must continue to prevail indefinitely, yet there can be nothing *absolutely* permanent about the formulation of a rational social liberalism. Such a liberalism is required only until the laws of all the sciences, including the science of society, come to be known, and it would be meaningless thereafter. But since at the moment no social theory occupies the status of law and all occupy the status of theory or hypothesis, liberalism must now apply unconditionally to all social studies. The goal of the ideal society is, of course, one in which all the laws of society are known, and in which the attitude of liberalism is not required. Of course this ideal is indefinitely remote and difficult of approach, so that little more can be expected than the very gradual establishment of social law and the correspondingly slow reduction of liberalism. Thus the criterion of progress in the social field as in all others is the extent to which the liberal attitude can reasonably be diminished, and not the reverse. Liberalism is strictly limited at both ends: it cannot be absolutely applied to all fields, since some laws have already been discovered by some sciences; yet it cannot be absolutely abolished short of the complete establishment of law. So far as the social sciences are concerned, liberalism is the attitude of hope assumed in the face of ignorance. It is thus actually an expedient measure taken as the best way to promote its own abolition.

The interim nature of rational social liberalism is inherent in the fact that human beings live in the historical order of actuality and are part of the actual world. They aspire to the complete reign of order, to the establishment of the logical order of possibility, yet are held down by the irreducible element of actuality and the partial nature of their own historical being. The predicament is recognized and made the basis for attack by those who oppose liberalism in all its forms. "A liberal," says that arch Catholic reactionary, Léon Daudet, "is a man who reveres God but respects the devil. He aspires to order and flatters anarchy in every domain." [5] The description is one which liberals may fairly accept. The liberal, in

[5] The Stupid XIX Century (Eng. trans., New York, 1928), p. 54.

other words, is one who wants to apprehend God yet give the devil his due. Philosophically, this means that the liberal wishes to achieve infinite value while remaining actual. But is this not true of all human beings? And does it not amount to a definition of the human being in all his aspiration and struggle? We may aspire to God, but to suppose that we can leave the devil behind altogether is to end by ceding everything to the devil, who takes a sure revenge whenever he is cheated of his portion. Those who have gone to such extremes of asceticism and renunciation as the Christian St. Anthony must recognize the truth of this assertion.

The point of liberalism in this regard is that without a certain amount of anarchy from time to time, the prevailing order can never become a wider order. This alternation from order to anarchy to order is part of the dialectic of actuality. Anarchy is necessary to increase the inclusiveness of order, and is evil only when taken as an end in itself. The liberal, then, is simply one who is not satisfied with any limited order but who wants always to keep open the possibility of greater order.

Individualistic liberalism cannot be saved, but must be supplanted by social liberalism. Does this mean that individualism has no validity whatsoever, and that it too must be overthrown? Not at all. It may be asserted definitely that individualism has an important place under the doctrine of social liberalism. Major advances in the apprehension of ideas, in science or wherever, are most frequently accomplished by individuals. Now, it is true that individuals do not work completely in isolation, and that their work should not end with them. The individual as a unit is only part of a social whole; but he is a real part, and as a part irreducible. In so far as it is individuals who serve society, the advance of society is impossible without the retention of a certain amount of freedom of thought, expression and action on the part of individuals.

Since liberation of the capacities of individuals for free, self-initiated expression is an essential part of the creed of liberalism, liberalism that is sincere must will the means that condition the achieving of its ends. Regimentation of material and mechanical forces is the only way by which the mass of individuals can be released from regimentation and consequent suppression of their cultural possibilities. The eclipse of liberalism is due to the fact that it has not faced the alternatives and adopted the means upon which realization of its professed aims depends. Liberalism can be true to its ideals only as it takes the course that leads to their attainment. The notion that organized social control of economic forces lies outside the historic path of liberalism shows that liberalism is still impeded by remnants of its earlier *laissez faire* phase, with its opposition of society and the individual. The thing which now dampens liberal ardor and paralyzes its efforts is the conception that liberty and development of individuality as ends exclude the use of organized social effort as means. Earlier liberalism regarded the separate and competing economic action of individuals as the means to social well-being as the end. We must reverse the perspective and see that socialized economy is the means of free individual development as the end.[6]

The old liberalistic doctrine of Bentham and the Mills assumed that liberty was the inalienable inheritance of the individual. But realistic social liberalism does not allow this to be held true. Realists, from Thomas Hill

[6] Dewey, *Liberalism and Social Action*, p. 90.

Green to Charles Peirce, have understood that liberalism is a goal and not the heritage of individuals.

> They [Green and his followers] served to break down the idea that freedom is something that individuals have as a ready-made possession, and to instill the idea that it is something to be achieved, while the possibility of the achievement was shown to be conditioned by the institutional medium in which an individual lives. These new liberals fostered the idea that the state has the responsibility for creating institutions under which individuals can effectively realize the potentialities that are theirs.[7]

Thus we see that for the individual to serve society there must be freedom for the individual, not as an atomic and self-contained unit, self-sufficient and absolutely free, but as a part of a larger whole, requiring as a part the necessary latitude to best perform its function for the whole. In this sense freedom becomes the irreducible minimum of liberalism under the realistic socialistic doctrine: the freedom to find the law and to follow it. Without the existence of an absolute and independent system of laws, which can be sought for and always approximated closer and closer in actuality, the conception of freedom has little meaning.

For realistic social liberalism is neither an ultimate nor an end, but exists for the sake of something else; and the recognition of this fact constitutes its chief virtue. When the end for the sake of which it exists is attained, it may be discarded. All men desire to know the truth, and they recognize that this way lies the good life; but truth concerning the social field is not yet known. Until it is known, freedom of thought and

[7] Ibid., p. 26.

expression is required for the sake of the hypotheses which must be formed in the search for that truth. When a social utterance (e.g., a political opinion) is voiced, and its contradictory is also voiced, we must be prepared to permit them both, although knowing that conflicting assertions cannot both be true. We allow them and reserve judgment, but only until such a time as we have a criterion for choosing between them. On that day, liberalism with regard to contradictory utterances may well be diminished, since there would no longer be any purpose served by allowing false assertions that are known as false, and demonstrably so, to be made.

The aim of liberalism which has made science possible is to preserve the pursuit of science by whatever means, until social science can obtain agreement in the social field, and make future opinionate differences on social matters an impossibility. As the abolition of the need for liberalism through the discovery of law is included in the ultimate goal of society, so the maintenance of a rational social liberalism is included in the proximate goal of society. We may conclude that if liberalism be understood as the old irrational individualistic liberalism, it may be abandoned, but that understood as rational social liberalism it must be retained.

PART III

PRACTICAL APPLICATIONS

10.

Liberal Democracy

Meets the Class Struggle

THE OBJECT OF THIS CHAPTER IS TO DISCOVER WHETHER the preservation of civil and economic liberties is possible in a free democracy under the stress of capitalistic monopoly. Will the advent of the class struggle in America prove fatal to the democratic form of government? Must freedom of speech, of the press, and of assembly, necessarily clash with freedom to maintain a decent economic standard? For the answers to these questions it will be necessary to undertake an examination of certain elements of our liberal government and more especially the theories which underlie them.

In this and the following chapter we shall seek to examine the more imminent aspects of the class struggle as it affects the outcome of American democracy. Chapter XII criticizes the general attitude underlying the American antipathy to theory, political theory as well as all other theory. It suggests that this attitude will have to be changed by a shift in the underlying philosophy if America under the democratic form of government is to hold its proper position in the world of nations. Chapter XIII concludes the book with an outline of what the ethics of the individual has been, and what it ought to be changed to if positive democracy is to prevail.

The Democratic Necessity for Pluralism

The maintenance of democracy is only possible under some system of political pluralism. By political pluralism is meant the absence in an organized state of any "single source of authority that is all-competent and comprehensive." Any separation of powers serves to avoid a single source of governmental authority. One example of political pluralism in America is the three-fold division of power into the legislative, executive and judicial, whereby an exact system of checks and balances is brought to the aid of just administration. Another example is the division of political control in the election system, so that two or more political parties struggle for power and none captures it permanently. Often one party elects the chief executive, while another has a majority in the legislature or judiciary. Under such a system, there is always assured a minority, or unsuccessful, political party making a plea for power in the future.

It is essential to the maintenance of the democratic form of government that the minority party, or parties, be enabled occasionally to wage a successful campaign, or at least be kept in the position of having its claims heard. The need for the prevention of the permanent capture of power by the party in control necessitates a strict and vigilant guarding of what are known as the civil liberties: freedom of speech, of the press and of assembly, as provided by the Constitutional Bill of Rights. Thus liberalism, as the civil liberties have come to be called, is essential to liberal democracy. Political pluralism can only be maintained where divergencies of interests are recognized politically, and corresponding platforms publicly and freely allowed.

This fact has long been acknowledged in America and the necessary provisions for it made accordingly. But there is another closely related fact which has not been sufficiently considered. Political pluralism most emphatically can *not* be maintained where divergencies of interests and platforms of contending parties are serious and fundamental. The balance between contending factions is impossible of continuance when these factions are divided on the solutions to problems of basic economic importance. This latter fact is what we are now facing in the challenge to American democracy. Before we examine the reasons behind this contention, however, it may be well to consider the history of the American political parties, in order to determine to what extent the statement has been true of them.

The division between American parties has always been drawn on broad economic lines. The programs and platforms of the major American parties have remained since their inception broadly consistent. With few exceptions, the rich merchants and industrialists have always rallied behind the old "Federalist-Whig" principles which still motivate their inheritors in the present-day Republican party. Likewise, the poor farmers and agriculturists have always rallied behind the old "Republican" principles which still motivate their inheritors in the present-day Democratic party. Thus at first glance there would appear to be a clash of economic interests between the two parties: the rich represented by the Federalist-Whig-Republicans, and their apologists, including such men as Hamilton, Webster and Seward;

and the poor represented by the Republican-Democrats, and their apologists, including such men as Jackson, Bryan, Theodore Roosevelt, and Wilson.

This first view by no means reveals the true situation. A glance at party platforms which have persisted is sufficient to demonstrate the comparative superficiality of those economic differences which are involved in the struggle between the parties. The current Republican party, under whatever name, has always stood for high tariffs and the encouragement of industry, for mercantile marine subsidies, international trade expansion, low (or no) income taxes, a strong central government and sound money. The current Democratic party, under whatever name, has always stood for low tariffs, the encouragement of commerce, currency inflation, the purchase of farm lands, the abolition of mercantile marine subsidies and strong states' rights. Thus far, although the issue is clear enough, party division along economic lines remains a minimal affair.

There must be considered still other affiliations and interests, loyalties which from time to time shifted the ground between the contending parties and prevented their division from ever assuming the sharp and bitter opposition between the rich and the poor. Sectional considerations provided one ameliorating factor. For example, the small Western farmers who owed their lands to earlier Republican grants though remaining poor have also remained faithful Republicans, whereas the rich southern planters who were large slave-owners sided with the Democrats. The Republican merchants and manufacturers through their opposition to slavery at one time found themselves in the strange rôle of defending the oppressed, and similarly the Democrats found themselves upholding aristocratic doctrine. Recently, the rise of the phenomena of competitive industries has thrown even some industrialists into the Democratic camp. The not uncommon practice of contributing to the campaign funds of both political parties in order to have a friend at court whoever happens to be king, has further obscured the issue. "In fact," says Beard, "every party is a more or less miscellaneous aggregation with a conservative right and a radical left, shading off into each other by imperceptible degrees." [1]

Perhaps the most significant factor in the whole account of American political parties is contained in the history of labor in politics. The effort at independent political action by labor dates back to the national convention of Labor Reformers held at Columbus, Ohio, in 1872, but all labor parties have either been short-lived or else have survived, like the American Federation of Labor, by means of the avowed policy of "keeping labor out of politics." Early it was discovered that traditional loyalties were already such as to render the successful pursuance of a separate political program for labor a hopeless task, and consequently a labor party did not seem a necessity. The adopted tactics of playing one major political party off against the other remained the only evidence of labor in politics.

This latter policy had the null effect of making it completely unnecessary for either political party to give any serious consideration to the petitionings of labor, and as a result labor was indeed kept out of politics. As a consequence, although detectable economic preferences exist in the two major political parties, the inertia of labor has

[1] Charles A. Beard, The American Party Battle (New York, 1928), p. 94.

prevented the class issue from becoming too sharply defined. The major American political parties have never been drawn up along lines consistent with the class struggle. Thus despite the extremism of certain notorious politicians the striving of the parties has never become bitter enough to render it untenable, and the balance of power between the alternately successful political parties has made it possible for the democratic form of government to be continuously maintained.

Recent economic events have decisively altered the political situation. The decline of the lower middle class together with the rapid rise of a class struggle constitutes a new challenge to our form of government. The increasing control of monopoly capitalism and the consolidation of a large industrial proletariat has in recent decades threatened to upset the democratic balance. The delicate adjustments of liberal democratic government are insufficiently strong to cope with the rigors of the class struggle. We could not hope to preserve the balance of the parties should the issues between them assume the mighty proportions of an economic class war. The minor differences between the parties rest on such major agreements that either party is willing to see the other in power for a time. But should class interests divide the parties, the success of either party must necessarily lead to the abolition of the other, because of its "revolutionary," or "reactionary," efforts to resort to other than fair electoral means to gain control. There can be no doubt that issues as fundamental as those represented by the fight between capitalist and worker inevitably bring about the appeal to force—a move which the party peacefully elected to power usually condemns as illegal. Thus the balance of power is destroyed by the armed retention, or armed seizure, of power; and the result is the obliteration of the losing party, which can never again make a bid for control.

There exist already today both extreme and moderate examples of such a development. In Russia, the capitalists have been completely annihilated, and can never again come into office. In Germany and Italy, on the other hand, the workers' parties have been disorganized; nothing short of a revolution now could put them in power. The workers in France have made some headway, but have not succeeded in destroying the organization of their enemies. It is fairly certain, however, that if the capitalists in France were to gain control under Doriot or La Rocque, the workers would never again be allowed to have a voice in the government. In general these changes are represented by the struggle between fascism and socialism. In a democracy, this opposition takes the form of a struggle between the executive and legislative branches of government.[2] The complete triumph of the legislative marks the success of socialism, whereas the complete triumph of the executive is equivalent to fascism.

Transferring the problem to our own country, it might be argued that if the Republicans were to become definitely the party of the rich and the Democrats the party of the poor, or if a third party were to arise, say a combination of the Committee for Industrial Organization in the East with the Farmer-Labor bloc in the West, which would force the Republicans over into an extreme conservatism, the liberal democracy under which we

[2] While the New Deal seems to be an exception to this statement, it is but one phase of a struggle for control. A Republican president in 1940 might bear out the contention.

have so long lived would be dangerously imperiled. The inevitable rule is that when party differences are of a serious economic nature, consisting for example of class distinctions, political pluralism breaks down because the party having temporary possession of the government will seek to perpetuate its power by means of the annihilation of the opposing party. Such action, lacking effective interference, must lead to the establishment of a political monopoly, a monistic dictatorship, and finally to the end of democracy.

The desire for political power is based on real economic interests, and so is generally widespread among all kinds and classes of people. It is impervious to the peculiar differences of temperament, of personality and character, and of subjective outlook in general. Those who have been deprived of, or have always lacked, political control, are jealous of those who wield it. Monopolistic dictatorship, as can be readily seen, is a form of government difficult to keep going without an alert vigilance. The expression of any opposition, however slight, however impotent, is interpreted as the hint of a threat which is capable of rapid growth. Hence monopolistic dictatorship must lead easily to the suppression of all civil liberties. Freedom of speech, freedom of the press, and freedom of assembly, are regarded as dangerous to its interests, and so they are condemned as weaknesses which the strength of absolute obedience supplants. Spartan hardihood, based on the nobility of want, is trumpeted to take the place of the lost economic liberty.

The monopolistic dictatorship of the workers destroys democracy and leads to the extermination of all opposition, as for example in Soviet Russia. The monopolistic dictatorship of the capitalists destroys democracy and leads to the extermination of all opposition, as for example in Germany. But the combination of capitalists with the middle class would seem to preserve democracy, as in America, and the combination of workers with the middle class would also seem to preserve democracy, as in France. The civil liberties cannot continue unless they have the support of the balance of power as held by political parties in a free democracy. But, likewise, the balance of power between political parties cannot continue without the support of the civil liberties.

We have tentatively concluded that the incursion of the class struggle in the midst of the democratic scene constitutes a challenge to the present form of government. How is this challenge to be met?

Can Pluralism Be Maintained?

Individualistic liberalism is the historic prerogative of capitalist society. The American democracy has been maintained despite the superimposition of a relative capitalist control over the application of its liberalist doctrinal platform. But in the inevitable struggle between capital and labor in the American democracy, a struggle which endangers the very form of democracy itself, the importance of capital must be somewhat abated. Individualistic liberalism, having been associated with capitalism, must suffer a like eclipse. Such an eventuality means to many socialists the end of liberalism; but this is not at all necessary. For, as we have noted, a social liberalism is possible, and moreover its future belongs with that of a workers' society. Liberalism faces the choice of having to maintain itself with the latter or of not surviving at all.

The separation of powers provided for by the American version of political pluralism takes many forms. Besides the division of central government into executive, legislative, and judicial branches, there is also the split between states' and national rights, and the further separation of powers involved in the unofficial two-party system. These structures are delicately balanced, and admittedly allow of many corruptions. For instance, we frequently find the judge acting as legislator, the executive as legislator, the judge as executive, and so on. The separation of powers does not provide for but suffers the abuse of powers; and there is no such thing as an absolute provision against such abuse. But the separation of powers as it has been interpreted in this country also provides the machinery for a workers' social democracy, a government of true representation and not of presumed authority, an administration of men seeking out proper and rational laws instead of one irrationally imposing laws upon men.

In the economic struggle, the issue of civil liberties though important is not of sole importance. What is sought for by the majority of the workers is not only the freedom to speak, to print, and to assemble, but also the freedom to eat. In other words, the masses want and feel that they have a right to demand a decent economic minimum. The workers' class is not primarily concerned to deprive other classes of their rights but only to restore the proper administration of the control of production. In the pursuance of this object, however, conflict arises and the cause of civil liberties is often neglected on both sides. Such an oversight may serve an immediate practicality (although even that is to be doubted), but it certainly defeats hope for the continuance of social progress. The freedom of the individual is essential to social progress, since the major social advances are always accomplished by individuals. The whole problem, then, is to preserve the civil liberties while maintaining also the right to a decent economic minimum: the combination of the freedom to speak with the freedom to work.

Finally formulated, the problem is as follows. Given the adverse conditions arising from capitalistic monopoly in a free democracy, to determine whether the preservation of civil and economic liberalism is possible. We have already noted that one solution consists in the establishment of a social liberalism. We have now to apply this doctrine to the more immediate question of whether or not the class struggle in America can be absorbed within the framework of our democratic government.

There appears to be only one way in which it will be possible to maintain liberal democracy under the stress occasioned by the revolt of labor against monopoly capitalism. Due to the quiescence of labor in the past, capitalists have remained in control of the two major parties. But as we have noted, this control was never absolute; it was merely relative. The major parties have obeyed the will of capitalism, but only within the severe bounds prescribed by the shifting opposition of the middle class. The Republicans never wanted Franklin D. Roosevelt to become President, and the capitalist bloc within the Democratic camp did not even want him chosen as their candidate. Yet he was chosen and elected, and re-elected despite the frantic cries of Wall Street. Now that labor is rising and presenting its demands in increasingly strong terms, however, the relative control of the major parties by capitalism no longer can be held proportionately to represent the people. If the class struggle is to be kept out of the party issue, the two major political parties have no recourse but eventually to adopt the workers' side of the class struggle. Should the workers, after all, choose to vote en masse, they would be the voting majority. If they were to combine with the middle class in order to control the two major parties, retaining some capitalistic representation in each, there might be some hope that liberal democracy would not have to be abandoned.

This would mean, in effect, that the major parties would have their minor differences, in the struggle over which they could continue to alternate in power. But it would prevent party representation of major differences, a situation inevitably fatal to liberal democratic government. On the list of doctrines which the major parties held in common, economic liberty would be added to the civil liberties, and jealously preserved, i.e., never made into a campaign platform. The freedom to eat could be founded on social liberalism, whereby an economic minimum would be made the prerogative of every individual. As for the civil liberties which have been so anxiously called into question today, they would be supported by a stronger American attitude toward discoverable principles. What could be put beyond the pale of individual opinion would be given public recognition as such; what could not would be left open to free opinion until such a time as agreement could be reached. Thus freedom of speech, of the press, and of assembly would be based on deeper postulates, on presuppositions which could be defended, and would not have to rest on the appeal to individual common sense or the doubting of the validity of all law.

The machinery to prevent the class struggle from entering into the party division in the United States is already in process of formation. We have the two parties, with their superficial doctrinal differences. We have the two vast labor groups, the American Federation of Labor and the Committee for Industrial Organization, the former with its old trade-union system and its Republican leanings, the latter with its broad labor program and its Democratic affiliations. Now, if the A.F. of L. were to swing with the Republican party, perhaps even to gain control of it by means of a new plan for active participation in politics, and the C.I.O. were to go with the Democratic party and perhaps take over its leadership, we would then see the same relative (but not absolute) control of the major political parties by labor which was formerly held by capital. This would still not amount to a dictatorship of any kind and would moreover preserve the democratic form of government.

There are those who will exclaim, "Would that it were not so!" when they see labor dictating the conditions which capital once laid down.[3] For them there is no answer. The point is that the choice and its solution are not matters of either judgment or individual taste. We have the issue with us, and it is up to us to meet it. But after all, why should we be so surprised that it is here? We have traced the history of the American party struggle, and we have seen that it never sharply rep-

[3] Others will fear that the split of labor will mean the continued control of capital. But provided the lower middle class can see its interests identified with those of labor, their fears must prove groundless.

resented class interests. This is true, but must not be taken to mean that there never was a class struggle in America.

The American Revolution was a class struggle, a struggle of American traders and farmers against the excessive taxes imposed by the British ruling class on its colonies. The American Constitution was drawn in a fashion calculated to preserve the interests of the Revolutionists while endeavoring to prevent the necessity for any similar occurrence in the future. But plantation owners rose, nevertheless, over the slaves, and traders over the free farmers. These were situations which democracy was able to settle without being dangerously shaken. Unfortunately for the cause of democracy and the balance of the class struggle, however, industrialism helped the traders to gain control over labor. Trade became large-scale industry, and trade and finance combined into monopoly capitalism, developments which showed the economic and the political struggles clearly as issues between capital and labor. Such a development was one which the framers of the Constitution were unable to foresee; hence they could not and did not provide for it.

Now, however, the issue is here, and there are two ways to meet it. If the attempt is made by allowing our major political parties to represent the interests of economic classes, the divergence will prove insupportable and democracy will collapse, with an attendant loss of civil liberties. But there is another alternative, one which will not permit the attainment of economic liberty to swamp these civil liberties which are so necessary to the furtherance of civilization. This alternative consists in splitting the labor vote between the two major parties. Thus we can substitute for a relative capitalistic control a relative labor control, while continuing to maintain the democratic form. But in this case we shall have our own democracy; and this, together with the righting of social and economic injustices, is what, from the viewpoint of the present work, is to be considered worthy.

To sum up our argument, the advent of the class struggle in America need not destroy liberal democracy, provided the basis of the civil liberties—freedom of speech, of the press, and of assembly—be changed from one of individualistic liberalism to one of social liberalism. What we have chosen to call economic liberty, or the freedom to work, can be combined with the civil liberties without the loss of the latter, if only the claims of labor are recognized by both the major political parties and the class struggle avoided as a major party issue. This would of necessity somewhat restrict the power of capital, just as the power of labor has been restricted in the past. But it is the price demanded for the preservation of our liberal democratic government, and it would seem to be worth while.

II.

Democracy and the Middle Class

THE PRINCIPAL EVENT IN THE POLITICAL FIELD OF THE present day is the development of several threatening alternatives to the democratic form of government. Before and again just after the war, democracy was disinterestedly militant; and it was hoped by the democratic nations that all those countries which had not yet adopted the constitution of democracy would do so at the earliest opportunity. Nothing could have been speedier than the destruction of this hope, and the reversal of the general Western tendency toward democracy. Even before the expectation had been given its widest utterance, Russia replaced her absolute monarchy with a communist government; and later the democratic drift in Italy and Germany had met with a sharp turn toward dictatorship. Thus the refusal to continue the democratic movement came from within as well as from without the democratic countries.

Long established political systems are vulnerable to the extent to which their principles come to be taken for granted without sufficient abstract understanding. Premises held so deeply they no longer need be explicitly attended to have a tremendous strength, and this is especially true in the case of political principles. The government whose fundamental laws are granted so wide an agreement that they never rise to the surface of controversy is the most stable of all. But, unfortunately, a certain run of unchallenged practicality deceitfully gives off the appearance of this same condition of ultimate agreement. It is only when new situations occur, situations which disturb the smooth operation of the system, that men are thrown back upon theoretical principles. And if the appearance of agreement does not truly represent implicitly accepted principles, then the prospects of a successful challenge to democracy are made possible.

It is fitting that those liberals whose beliefs have been responsible for their expulsion from dictatorships and who have sought refuge in the firmest of democracies should be the most concerned with the definitions and methods of preservation of democratic principles. In a symposium just published[1] they have sought to consider the most theoretical as well as the most practical aspects of the topic in question. Since we here in America are living through a "time of troubles," to use Professor Toynbee's phrase, it is a question which lies close to the interests of every American. Thus the authors of this work have rendered us a service of which we cannot be unmindful. In what follows we shall endeavor to avail ourselves both of their inquiries and their results, but for the particular cast of the argument as well as for the conclusions from the evidence offered they are not responsible. In reading the thread of the reasoning presented in these assorted essays, a certain collective logic had to be presupposed, and this has necessitated a particular shift of emphasis for which it is not fair to hold the authors responsible.

[1] *Political and Economic Democracy*, eds. Max Ascoli and Fritz Lehmann (New York, 1937).

"The goal [of democracy] is to attain on every political issue the greatest possible autonomy, security and expectation of improvement for individuals and for groups, without other limitations than mutual compatibility." [2] "Liberal ideology confined the state to the duty of watching the rules of the game; it was believed that the goals of the game, the values which make the life of man in society worth while, would be realized through social automatism." [3] The system allowed for the greatest possible freedom with the least amount of restriction. It also allowed for the rapid growth and culmination of contradictory situations whose solution in any direction worked for the overthrow of the democratic principles which had allowed them the freedom to operate. Let us touch upon a few of the most important of these situations.

We have been living under the system of political democracy, but economic inequalities arise to challenge the very idea of democracy by the enormity of its discrepancies. "Economic policy is after all policy—policy with an economic object. This part of state policy cannot be left to the decision of the particular interests involved, any more than can any other part of that policy." [4] Too late in the day of maladjustment it has been learned that the right to eat is as important a part of the individual's basic requirements as the right to vote. The challenge to the functioning of our own government has taught us that economics and politics are closely interwoven, that economic democracy is as much democracy as is political democracy.

[2] Ibid., p. 15.
[3] Ibid., p. 23.
[4] Ibid., p. 187.

Another contradiction, closely related to the above, is one that occurs between the free interplay of economic forces and a certain measure of control. The free interplay of economic forces is maintained out of political democratic principle; the certain measure of control is a consequence of the exigencies of actual emergency. Thus both appear to be required, yet they are mutually exclusive. There has never been a time when the American government did not exercise a certain measure of control. With the appearance of sharp economic inequality, the condition has become aggravated. The contradictory situation is well illustrated in the Sherman Act. "The Sherman Act represents a policy which, though it refuses to have economic life regulated by a central authority, nevertheless does not leave the fate of society to the free play of allegedly existing rules of nature." [5]

Democracy as the guardian of the rules of the game is restricted from interfering with any changes that may take place in the game itself in the course of economic development. Thus anti-democratic forces have sought to hamper the rise of trade unions by making considerable concessions to the status of the worker. Such concessions are interpreted by the intelligent trade unionists as a blow aimed at their democratic liberty. The only defense they have against monopoly capital is organization, and such concessions as compulsory arbitration, while improving the economic position of the worker somewhat, are actually Greek gifts. "The union loses its principal function, collective bargaining, and its right to strike, and as a compensation is obliged to see to the enforcement of the award for the non-observance of

[5] *Ibid.*, p. 108.

which it can be made liable." [6] Democracy can only be preserved on the basis of a balance between subsidiary forces within its borders; yet it is powerless to interfere even to the extent of seeing the balance maintained. Thus it is prohibited from insuring its own continuance.

Economic inequality itself builds up capitalism to the point where the latter's existence is threatened. There is a natural limit to the size of an organization in any field. In the political and economic field capitalism has brought about the development of organizations so vast that their internal relations are threatened and they become outwardly vulnerable as well. In addition, the rise of monopoly capital tends to replace the very conditions of competition which have made the existence of capitalism possible. The problem is perhaps most marked in the case of the ownership of public utilities. The issue is really one of the preservation of capitalism versus the existence of such a phenomenon as monopoly capital.

The same difficulties prevail in agriculture that we have found in industry. One contradiction in agriculture is between the small family-co-operative farm and the large-scale farm. The influence of such vitally important new conditions as the development of farm machinery has made the contradiction a flat one. Again, the effect of a magnified industrialism upon agricultural life has been to produce in the latter a one-sided discrepancy: there are few farm magnates but many farm paupers. Agricultural as well as industrial success is hampered under capitalism by the contradiction between consumer and producer. Every employed individual is to some extent both; and yet the disparity between the two interests,

[6] Ibid., p. 88.

due in large part to an emphasis upon production for profit rather than use, is enormous.

Such are the economic phases of our present-day democratic contradictions; but the struggle is by no means confined to the economic level. Perhaps the economic sphere is originally to blame for occasioning the upset, but at least we may say that the struggle has penetrated to the point where purely political contradictions are in evidence. There are four separate instances of this which are clearly discernible.

The first consists in the fact that the demand for democratic representation is along lines no longer conformable with the representation for which traditional provision was made. The rise of industrialism and its usurpation of majority prerogatives, the exaggerated development of the divisions of labor, also fostered by industrialism, have led to the demand for occupational representation. The representation provided for by the traditions of our democracy are largely geographical and numerical, and this representation wars with the new demand for occupational representation. Thus we have a contradiction, of a political nature, between class organizations insisting upon representation as such, on the one hand, and upon local representation on the other. Rapid communications and the power tool have brought about a closer central control, and occasioned the demand for representation exactly by interests rather than roughly by location.

The ability of representative government to act with sufficient unanimity and promptitude has lately become suspect. Members of parliaments far from being cross-sections of the population are consistently low grade; yet they enjoy authority. They hamper as well as help governmental activity; yet they modify its extreme decisions.[7] Under parliamentarism, mediocrity follows compromise, and bafflement discussion. Each member becomes a pleader for special interests, and the collective voice is hardly raised for the collective good. Certainly representative government was not designed to meet emergency, yet this is just what it does have to meet, and therein lies a contradiction which was always latent but not until recently painfully in evidence.

The whole question, to which democracy yields no answer and over which it takes no sides, is the question of individualism versus collectivism. The belief is that democracy leans toward individualism; but this is ruled out by the fact that individualism never was and cannot be absolute. There has been always in democracies a measure of collective control; and even apart from governmental interference the individual has usually had to rely upon group solidarity of some sort, whether regional, occupational or whatever.

In some ways the most desperate issue of all is not between candid individualism and collectivism, but rather involves these same interests on a much broader scale. Its widest presentation is under the names of democracy and nationalism. Democracy rose historically with nationalism, but today its survival is a question transcending national boundaries. "The nationalist dictatorships have no use for the liberal identification of internal and external freedom, of self-determination and equality. Some of them have used these slogans, but for external use only and with a definite alteration of their moral and

[7] *Ibid.*, p. 202.

political value. Also there are democracies with no special nationalist mythology, such as the Scandinavian
countries. Democracy today is uneasy about nationalism." [8] The fact that a democracy is nationalized ham-
pers its political decisions. Any distinctions between
democracies, such as trade barriers and racial immigra-
tion barriers, are essentially undemocratic. Democracy
rose historically with nationalism and was for a time
aided by it, but is far more inclusive and logically independent.

The contradictions which we have enumerated constitute the moments of stress of our democracy. Can it
survive them? A significant indication in this regard is
the fact that most of the essays in the work in question
point out that for each of the contradictions allowed
under democracy there are offered two radical solutions:
those of communism and fascism. Both involve, of
course, the abandonment of democracy. Confined to
"the duty of watching the rules of the game," democracy
is in danger of being rendered powerless to prevent the
utter disruption of the game itself, a disruption which
is fast taking place by means of the intensification of the
struggle between the players. Can an effective democracy be saved? The answer to this question is, as we
shall see, implicit in the form of the contemporary social
struggle.

From the nature of the contradictions we have been
examining, it is apparent that democracy is threatened
economically from the top and from the bottom. The
inequalities of wealth are more than any liberal democracy can bear. "Without claiming accuracy it is safe to

[8] *Ibid.*, p. 308.

say that in 1930 the wealthiest 2 per cent of the population owned at least 40 per cent of all private wealth." [9] This concentration of wealth means an even greater concentration of power. It means, most significantly of all, that some eight hundred oligarchical families are enabled to oppose some six to ten millions of industrial workers. The industrial workers by means of efficient organization and leadership challenge the exclusive control of the means of production by the owning class. This brings about a class war, in which not over a third of the total population is involved but which nevertheless threatens to disrupt altogether the democratic form of government.

The middle class remainder of the population is enlisted in support of one side or another in the conflict. When the majority of the middle class takes sides, the result is some variety of socialism or fascism; socialism when the middle class sides with the workers, fascism when it sides with the finance capitalists. Thus if the economic struggle between labor and monopoly capital it to be taken as final, with the middle class torn between them, democracy is of necessity doomed. The top and the bottom of the social strata threaten democracy; only the middle class makes an effort to hold on to a kind of government from which it has received benefits in the past and from which alone it could hope to receive greater benefits in the future. For if it takes sides in the class struggle, its interests are scuttled by partisanship. The monopoly capitalist is engaged in destroying the means of existence of a middle class by his very engagement in monopoly. The worker asks for a dictatorship in which the manual laborer is supreme. Neither

[9] *Ibid.*, p. 162.

monopoly capital nor manual labor can win control without enlisting the aid of the middle class. Yet the middle class does not stand to benefit by either dictatorship but only by economic and political democracy.

Democracy is inevitably identified with the middle class, as it has been from Aristotle's day to this.[10] The salvation of democracy hangs upon the willingness and ability of the middle class to make some attempt to resolve the extremes of economic inequality and to clear up the political confusions which prevail at the present time. As to the economic inequality, "If the property of the wealthiest tenth of the population in the United States were distributed among the whole population, the property of the average man would be tripled."[11] America is certainly wealthy enough to support the demands of such a democracy, but all depends upon some kind of equable distribution, and this is the task of the middle class whose very economic status is capable of serving as a norm. The chief danger of democracy today consists in the fact that the middle class lacks both solidarity and leadership. Democracy is threatened from the left and from the right because of this defection of the leadership of the middle class, which is the logical bulwark of democracy.

Some hint of what kind of solution to the prevailing difficulties at the political level can be offered by the middle class is contained in the distinction between the rule of men and the rule of law. Democracy took its rise in the assumption, inherited from the fight against absolute theology, that government by law is restrictive whereas government by men is liberating. But as a mat-

[10] *Ibid.*, pp. 260–61.
[11] *Ibid.*, p. 164.

ter of record, just the opposite has proved to be the case. Government by men instead of law develops a body of laws which are restrictive, whereas true government by law, which is to say government by men in search of the true law which they know to exist as a possibility, is liberating. "The principle of justice and reason as opposed to arbitrary dealing is not only chronologically earlier than the people-principle against the king-principle, it is likewise structurally [i.e., logically] primary." [12] In other words, if political democracy is to be retained, the undemocratic government by men whose regulations are restrictive of minorities (or of majorities, for that matter) in favor of vested interests, must be abandoned for more democratic law. And in operation democratic law consists in the method exemplified when men attempt to find the truth in terms of which laws can be framed.

Laws are the rules of the democratic game. They are found by men in search of the truth in terms of which there can be rules, not by men eager for ruling. Men may rule; but it is reason which should rule the rulers. Reason is the final authority in the political sphere as well as in other forms of orderly procedure, as for instance physical science. Understood in this way, democracy appears as the rough attempt to put scientific method to work in the political and economic, or social, field. In the choice between law as restrictive and law as liberating there should be but one alternative. The rule of men is restrictive, but the rule of law is liberating. Thus democracy should be the organization of men ruling by means of tentative regulations but constantly working to discover and to put into effect the govern-

[12] Ibid., p. 278.

ment of freedom by law.   In this way, democracy would develop an organization with its emphasis on inclusion rather than exclusion.   It would lose its rigid and un-compromisingly nationalistic character, and become a step on the road toward the international brotherhood of mankind.   Nothing finite is final, and democracy can serve its highest purpose by uniting under common bonds of interest and sympathy all those who acknowledge the rule of reason.

12.

The Future of American Practice

WHEN WILLIAM JAMES SPOKE OF "THE ATTITUDE OF looking away from first things, principles, 'categories,' supposed necessities; and of looking towards last things, fruits, consequences, facts," [1] he adopted a position which was well justified by the American life of his day. His philosophy gave official voice to the prevailing scorn for theory and respect for practice, a viewpoint which has known of no exceptions for good theories and bad practices. Indeed so deeply is this position held that it is not even maintained; it has come down to the expedient procedure of acting first and thinking about the consequences of actions afterward.

To be American has always meant to be eminently practical. What have we in common, if not our practicality? We are hard-headed; we have a way of getting things done. Notoriously not idle dreamers but busy people who prefer to act rather than to discuss, to accomplish rather than to contemplate, we are alive to the good things of the present and also the great possibilities of the future. We do not, we insist, want to waste our time in doing nothing, while the sun shines and the earth smells and it is good to be alive. For we are keenly aware of the pleasures of mere existence; and we

[1] *Selected Papers on Philosophy* (Everyman ed.), p. 204.

love, above all, our own power and our striving. We love to see the products of our labors in some way visible; we like having tangible results. We watch with admiration and the solid feeling of achievement, as the railroads we have built stretch across the country, the ships we have made stand out to sea, and the continent we have conquered lies prostrate at our feet.

This attitude has helped us a long way forward. Certainly there is no question but what American technology is thus far the best in the world. The applications of the findings of physical and of biological science to the furtherance of man's practical requirements and ends is accomplished in America with more dexterity and dispatch than it is in any other civilized country. Our bridges, our skyscrapers, our airplanes and our hospitals are more expertly constructed than those of other peoples; they function more efficiently. We are sensible; we face issues squarely. We are afraid of nothing but remain just what we are: self-contained and (as we like to think) wholly self-sufficient.

But where did we find the technology; where did we get the issues? Did we start from the earliest beginnings, or in the middle of things?

For years we were so busy making office boys into presidents and little industries into big ones, so busy beating last year at whatever cost and by whatever means, that we did not see the great depression coming. Once it arrived, the immediate and urgent problems of salvaging whatever could be salvaged, and of girding up our loins for the restoration of some semblance of order, was so terribly upon us, that we had no time for any other thoughts or pursuits. We dared not look backward or forward, but used up all our strength during the long pause in setting out to gain another burst of speed. Only recently has it been possible to consider that, although the practical thing is the American thing, and the practical must follow from theories of some sort, there is no such thing as an American theory of any considerable dimensions and scope.

A discouraging thought, yet let us face the facts bravely, as earnest Americans when they are called upon can do. What makes our lack of advanced theories so disastrous is that all practice must be deduced from theory of some sort. Theory can exist without its practice, though in this case, to be sure, it is not of much value. But practice cannot get along without theory. Industrial technology is the practice which follows from the theories of pure science. Practical issues, whether those of economics, politics, or whatever, must be the application of general theories in those special fields.

Now, the simple fact is that all American practice follows from previously established European theories. Faraday could work on the dynamo without any help from the General Electric Company, but the very existence of the General Electric Company would have been inconceivable without the previous theoretical investigations of Faraday and others. The broad conceptions of Newton, of Einstein, of Freud, are all European. Our political system of democracy is European, having been derived from the writings of Locke and Montesquieu; and now the two proffered alternatives of fascism and communism are also European. It is fair to say that America has never given birth to a single great and fruitful conception in any of the sciences, whether natural or social. This is an unfortunate fact, but it is a fact nevertheless, and as such it will have to be dealt with.

Very recently, one investigator [2] thought that it might be instructive to write a popular book, giving to those who have no familiarity with the technical languages of the sciences an opportunity to know what was taking place in the frontiers of scientific research. Accordingly he made a tour of the scientific laboratories throughout the United States. Some thirty odd in all were visited; physical, biological, and psychological. His investigations led him to the discovery of a very startling conclusion, one which was detrimental to the cause which he was espousing.

In any one of the larger laboratories which he had the opportunity of visiting, he discovered first of all that there was more money spent on research and more highly-trained men devoting themselves to science, than in almost all the corresponding European laboratories in the same field. Despite this superiority of opportunity, however, he found not a single instance of the broad general conceptions of science, no Einsteins at work, no Darwins, no Freuds. The latter half of Jaffe's work is a serious and unanswerable indictment of American tendencies in scientific research.[3] Even our twelve Nobel Prize winners, as he points out, received the award for "manual dexterity rather than broad theory." In short, he was unable to discover any large-scale figures actively engaged in the pursuit of theoretical science in America; he found no scientists of a stature sufficient to enable them to stand beside the greatest that Europe has produced and still produces.

[2] Bernard Jaffe, *Outposts of Science* (New York, 1935), p. xxii.
[3] *Ibid.*, pp. xxi–xxvi.

The development of American theory continues to lag some distance behind the accomplishments of American practice. In effect, this can mean but one thing. If the contention is true, and if it can definitely be proved that theory and practice are interrelated, and that all practice must follow from theories of one sort or another, then, at least until we have been able to develop theories of our own, we shall be helplessly dependent in our practice upon the theories sent over from the abstract speculations of Europeans. This has certainly been the case in the past; but does it necessarily have to be true of the future as well? There is little doubt that we are capable of becoming as independent of Europe for our ideas as we have been for their applications. To show this, it will be necessary first to ask why we have always been so averse to abstract theory.

Our native antipathy to theory has been natural enough, and can be explained quite easily. It has two sources, the first of which lies in the historical origins of the American adventure in civilization. The Americans who constructed America in a physical sense—those who made the cities, wrote the textbooks, and are responsible in a general way for the color of American life—came from Europe. Logically, therefore, they took their influences from European accomplishments. Now, immigrants have, so to speak, to travel light; being unable to transport everything, it is necessary for them to take only those things which are immediately needed. What, in good faith, could be more necessary to a pioneer civilization than an efficient and advanced technology? Since what was most sorely required was the practical application of a technology, the Americans ingenuously took over European scientific theories and deduced from them an American technology which proved better and more advanced.

Because we are an essentially practical people, and deem it forthright to see as important what is immediately present, we have looked to practice much more than we have to theory. To put the matter bluntly, theories are spun in somebody else's mathematical tables. These cannot so easily be understood as having the utmost practical importance. On the other hand, practices, together with their results, are plainly material. Skyscrapers are tangible and visible (and pretty much so at that), whereas the stress and strain calculations that have made them possible are buried away somewhere in somebody's book on the principles of mechanical engineering. And so because our materialism is of a naive kind we tend to scoff at the mathematics and to concentrate on the skyscrapers, derogating theory in favor of its attendant practice.

The second reason for our present plight is not very far removed from the first. More abstractly, the prevailing American philosophy of pragmatism, or the worship of the practical, may be held accountable. William James is our great philosopher, not because he originated anything, but because he was able to run his hand over the contours of the American skull and in this way tell what was going on in its brain. He was very much alive to American currents of thought and feeling; and he accepted them as his own gospel. Philosophy is the search for truth, and James identified truth with immediate practicality.[4] Peirce, the teacher

[4] E.g., William James, *Pragmatism* (New York, 1907), p. 48: ". . . meaning, other than practical, there is for us none." But what about the truth of "if-then" propositions whose meaning is in no wise dependent upon application? James would rule out the whole of

of James, had pointed out that practicality follows from truth.[5] Peirce meant that what is practical works be-cause it is true, and not the reverse.[6] But James was looking out toward the common trend and not listen-ing very intently. As a consequence, he got Peirce's doctrine twisted around to the notion that truth follows from practicality. This was a very quaint notion in-deed; but oddly enough it seemed at the time to suit the American people, who were desirous of having a justification for their emphasis on practicality. How convenient to have one in the form given by James, to be able to believe that in their search for practicality they were really searching for the abstract theory of truth!

The changes that occur in a run of time have a way of rubbing the paint from smooth surfaces, thus enabling us to penetrate to the contradictions which lie beneath. The practical proves the true, not because the practical is true, but because the true is practical. Largely on account of the failure to understand this principle, the remorseless logic of events has brought about the bank-ruptcy of pure speculation in America, and left us help-lessly dependent upon Europe to furnish the abstract theories which we can proceed to put into concrete prac-tice.

Some unexpected confirmations of this fact have ap-peared. It so happens that these are taken from de-velopments which have recently occurred in scientific laboratories. There are two kinds of such laboratories in America: foundation or university laboratories, and

logica docens and leave as valid only logica utens, which is only half of logic.

[5] Collected Papers, 5.9.

[6] Ibid., 5.403.

industrial laboratories. The first group are supposedly devoted to the furtherance of pure scientific research, for instance the Rockefeller Institute for Medical Research; the second are erected by large industrial corporations for the useful purpose of perfecting techniques, and of devising inventions which can be patented, produced and sold for profit, for instance the Du Pont Laboratories. A glance at developments in both kinds will yield a very instructive moral.

Recently several men who have been given grants in aid to pursue research in the physical and biological sciences, by endowed foundations and prominent universities, have said, very confidentially of course, that, although they were supposed to be working on pure science, the authorities brought unofficial and delicate but none the less firm pressure to bear on them to produce something more practical. A result which could be of immediate social benefit, one which could be advertised, or one which could be turned to cash profit, was wanted; something, in any case, which would bring public attention and prestige to the institution. The scientists remarked that direct emphasis on every one of these ends was detrimental to the pursuit of pure science. Whatever pure science they did succeed in producing had perforce to be kept more or less under cover and developed surreptitiously. Inquiry into the reason for this state of affairs produced the information that the authorities in charge of these institutions really had held the utmost scorn for pure or theoretical science, and secretly envied the industrial laboratories which were reputedly so free of that sort of idle speculation.

It was with great eagerness, then, that the inquiry turned toward the industrial laboratories, and scientists were questioned in order to learn how they were faring. The particular history of the elaborate laboratories maintained by one corporation in upper New York state well illustrates the point. This corporation some while ago had desired to improve and elaborate upon its product, and so had brought over a few skilled technicians from Europe and put them to work. These men, however, were technicians; they knew how to do what they were supposed to do with the utmost skill; but they emphatically did *not* know how to improve their technique or change their product. The directors of the laboratories accordingly concluded that the imported technicians were too "practical," and that what was required was men with more knowledge of the abstract theory involved. Technicians were accordingly secured who knew something of the relevant mathematical theory. But, alas, they also proved too practical, and could do little besides experiment in the laboratory with the equipment with which they were already familiar.

The second group did, however, accomplish a little more than the imported technicians. Spurred on by this partial success, and now well on the track of the correct procedure, the directors of research next decided to hire mathematical specialists, men scornfully referred to in the science of chemistry as "pencil chemists" because they do little or no laboratory work with actual chemical compounds but concentrate instead upon the complicated mathematical formulae of chemistry with paper and pencil at a desk. With this last group some progress in research is finally being made. The salaries of these "pencil chemists" are being amortized over a long period, and the corporation regards their employment as an investment, promising the likelihood of great practical and financial returns in the future.

Observe the amazing moral! While the laboratories of theoretical science, scornful of theory, are turning more and more to the search for immediate practical results, the laboratories of practical industry are being forced to become more and more abstract and theoretical —solely as a practical and expedient measure. The scientific failure of the foundations is being compensated by the industries themselves. What a travesty on science this represents: an anomalous situation brought about by our failure to recognize the concrete practicality of abstract theory!

Outside those western European countries in which modern science took its start, the situation is much the same as it is in America. In the Russian philosophy, for example, the unity of theory and practice is well understood. Let us then take a glance at the progress of Soviet science, in order to see whether the Russian situation is any better than our own.

Upon analyzing the progress of science in Russia, we see at once that there another variation of our difficulty prevails. Russia, when the Soviets came into power, was an industrially backward country. In their efforts to develop the technology and natural resources of that country, the Soviets, too, have been forced to an over-emphasis upon immediate practicality.[7]

They, however, have had a philosophy which insists upon the unity of theory and practice. But their philosophy commits a serious mistake in this regard. For

[7] Cf. the preoccupations of the Soviet scientists, as reported by an English observer who was obviously prejudiced in their favor, J. G. Crowther, Soviet Science (London, 1936).

the unity of theory and practice in the communist philosophy depends upon the simultaneity of the occurrence of such theory and practice in time. Since the communists do not believe that "pure" science is possible at all, they are led to insist that practice must follow hard upon theory, lest the theory seem too "pure." In practice, this has brought about the absurdly naive procedure of building industrial factories and scientific laboratories under the same roof.

In conformity with dialectical materialism, Crowther insists that "theory and practice are inseparable, and neither has scientific meaning without the other." [8] Despite his effort to make out a good case for the progress of science in Russia, despite a long catalogue of technological experimentations now going on, he is forced to admit that "progress in scientific research apparently depends on the invention of scientific ideas, and not directly on the invention of ingenious apparatuses" [9] and that "the part of communist scientists is at present more prominent in applied than in pure science." [10] The gap is plain enough. The plea of extenuating circumstances is to some extent, of course, validated. Soviet Russia must industrialize. But even here, the necessity of keeping up with the advance of the major industrial nations involves a certain amount of concentration on what has been scornfully referred to as "pure" science.

But those who depend upon the habit of having a messenger boy waiting in the laboratory for something to be discovered which can be rushed over to the factory

[8] *Op. cit.*, p. 5.
[9] *Ibid.*, p. 46.
[10] *Ibid.*, p. 22.

and there immediately produced in large quantities for mass consumption, are doomed to disappointment. Abstract science is not served in this way, and neither is concrete practicality. The development from scientific theory to technological practice is a comparatively slow process. What the Russians have thus far failed to realize is that the unity of theory and practice is not itself a practice but a theory which is capable of having practical effects.

In America, it has been often affirmed in recent times that the frontier is closed. Our country has been built, as much as it can be built, following upon the practical application of abstract scientific principles developed in Europe. But quite a change has come upon the Western mood in recent years. Europe is tired, and we are young. We should not look across the water for guidance any longer. Perhaps now it is our turn to assume the leadership.

Of what, in the last analysis, does such leadership consist? Not in the effort to apply a technology more successfully than anyone else. Not in the ability to face grave issues squarely and to come to a steady opinion concerning them. Leadership, in the highest sense of which we are speaking, lies rather in the ability to think one's way through to the formulation of theoretical science, and to the abstract principles of social, political and economic theory. We must develop our respect for and capacity to indulge in theoretical speculation of the utmost abstraction. For it is this kind of speculation, governed by reference to fact, which eventually leads to the greatest practicality. Only so shall we learn how to become completely independent of Europe, and self-sufficient in the fullest sense. Only so shall we develop the qualities and capacities for self-leadership which can carry us forward toward the future of immense practicality of which the world stands so desperately in need.

In the new America, with its closed frontiers and its new need for consolidation, the interpretation put upon pragmatism by William James can no longer play any important rôle. It has had its day; but now we can no longer despise as he did the whole lot of "first things, principles, and 'categories.'" To be sure, the necessity that he saw is still with us, the logical obligation to stick to the facts in order to be sure that we are on the right track, to seek for "last things, fruits, consequences." We have learned a lesson with regard to speculation for its own sake as an end; and we know that this too involves a division of theory and practice. We shall never return to the kind of speculation which was carried on in the later Middle Ages, because we know that theory has its consequences in practical action. But we can no longer make the vicious division that James made. For the unity of theory and practice requires the encouragement of theory as an aid to practice.

Our opportunity to lead not only ourselves but the whole of world development lies waiting. It requires that we restore due importance to theory, as being required for practice, and that we pursue the independent development of theory before we attempt to deduce any practical effects from it. It is true that there are some abstract theories which lead to no practice, but there are others which do, and it is the latter we mean by theory. In general it may be stated that only false theories lead to no valid practice. True theories are always eventually practical. Abstract theory is of the first importance; concrete practice is not always so easy to deduce, but cannot be deduced at all unless it has been preceded by some theory. It is the theoretical Americans who have been offered the opportunity of being the lords of the future. That is what our energy and enterprise is for; that is the meaning of our destiny.

13.

The Rational Democratic Ethics

of Peirce

Peirce's Pragmatic Doctrine of Truth

IF IT IS TRUE THAT DEMOCRACY AS WE HAVE HAD IT HAS been conceived as resting on a nominalistic and hence negative and irrational basis, it must at least be admitted that the ethics, both implicit and acknowledged, of such a democracy has been consistent with its foundations. In our expanding economy, in which new fields of endeavor have been made available to the adventurous individual almost faster than they could be utilized, the ethics of Jamesian pragmatism has had its effect in fact as well as in a loudly proclaimed doctrine. This doctrine as well as the practice from which it was deduced were perfectly consistent with negative democracy. But it will be shown that positive democracy as we have outlined it in the foregoing chapters demands another kind of ethics, a rational ethics more suited to democracy than the ethics of Jamesian pragmatism. It will be proposed that this ethics which has gone unnoticed has already been supplied by another American philosopher, Charles S. Peirce.

It is our first task, then, to examine the pragmatic ethics of William James. This we can do best, perhaps, by first stating Peirce's doctrine of truth, since James candidly took Peirceian pragmatism as his starting point; it will then be possible to show how the doctrine of James constituted a deviation.

It was to be expected that a philosopher who had exposed the error of nominalism, studied scholastic realism and made himself familiar with the aims and methods of experimental science, would attempt to put realism and science together. The result was Peirce's doctrine of pragmatism, a theory of the relation between truth and practicality, defined methodologically as follows: "In order to ascertain the meaning of an intellectual conception one should consider what practical consequences might conceivably result by necessity from the truth of that conception; and the sum of these consequences will constitute the entire meaning of the conception." [1] There are two important points which should be noted at once about this definition. In the first place, Peirce says that the practical consequences of a conception "result by necessity from the truth of that conception." Thus while truth and practicality are indissolubly associated, and some acquaintance with practicality is essential in order to ascertain the complete meaning of truth, still it is truth which determines practicality, and not the reverse. Indeed, Peirce specifically says that the practical consequences result by necessity from truth. In the second place, we may observe that it is not the mere consequences as random affairs which constitute the

[1] *Collected Papers*, 5.9.

meaning of a conception, but the *sum* of the consequences. Now, to ascertain the sum of the practical
consequences of a conception, an infinite run of actuality
is required, since anything less than an infinite actuality
could not produce "the *sum* of the consequences."

That the doctrine of pragmatism as designed by Peirce
was intended to aid in the avoidance of the Scylla of
extreme realism as well as the Charybdis of nominalism,
is evident in many passages. Nominalism is ruled out
by the contention that generals are real. But are *all*
generals real? No, for this is the error which is the opposite of nominalism: the fallacy of extreme realism. To
assert that all generals are real, without ascertaining the
degree of their self-consistency and their range of applicability, must mean, in some cases at least, to set up
falsehoods as truths, which in turn implies generals to
be unrelated to actuality. Not all general objects are
real, says Peirce, but only "some general objects are real.
(Of course nobody ever thought that *all* generals were
real; but the scholastics used to assume that generals
were real when they had hardly any, or quite no, ex-
periential evidence to support their assumption; and
their fault lay just there, and not in holding that generals
could be real.)"[2] Pragmatism as Peirce designed it is
the device by which the reality of generals is to be as-
certained. It is the doctrine according to which practical consequences are to be observed with a view to
determining just what truths those consequences are
following by necessity.

Peirce's logic proves to be that logic of pragmatism
wherein the requirement of an infinity of consequences
is made plainly evident. Peirce avoided the realistic

[2] *Ibid.*, 5.430.

fallacy by demanding the practical consequences of his truths to exemplify and illustrate them, holding as he did that any truth which could not develop into action could not be truth. He avoided the fallacy of nominalism by asserting the reality of truth which practical consequences must follow by necessity but do not create. In his pragmatic theory of truth, he identified truth and practicality but made the latter depend upon the former for its validity and made the former depend upon the latter for its demonstration.

The Ethics of William James

Since the understanding of the realistic doctrine of pragmatism as set forth by Peirce has been somewhat altered by William James, and since it is James who deserves the credit for making the doctrine generally known, it will be our task next to indicate the deviation. Peirce and James each deduced an ethics from the Peirceian pragmatic theory of truth, but the two systems of ethics which they deduced are contradictory. Peirce's ethics is consistent with his truth-theory; James' ethics is not.

In a volume devoted to the topic of pragmatism, James first acknowledges Peirce as his source and then proceeds to expatiate on the implications to ethics of his own interpretation of pragmatism. Pragmatism, for James as for Peirce, is a theory of truth; it is also a way of discovering truths. But James' version, unlike Peirce's, is anti-intellectualistic, and so looks away from abstractions, absolutes, fixed principles, and closed systems; it is practical and so looks toward facts, concreteness and action. According to Jamesian pragmatism, "the only test of probable truth is what works best in the way of leading us." His pragmatism "can see no meaning in treating as 'not true' a notion that was pragmatically successful." On the ethical side we may note the same divergence. In real life when truths clash with "vital benefits" it is the truths which must be dismissed. If actions which seem demanded clash with principles, then, says James, he takes a "moral holiday." [8] For justification, the moral holidays are either just brazenly taken, or else as a philosopher James says he tries to justify them by some other principle.

In dealing with first principles of philosophy, we are at so fundamental a level that the slightest deviation of doctrine, the most infinitesimal difference in interpretation, may allow for divergent chains of implications which end by directly contradicting each other. Thus men may start from almost the same metaphysics yet in general appear to hold deeply opposed philosophies. Peirce said that what works works because it is true; James said that what is true is true because it works. By just the slightest shift of emphasis, James brought the Peircean doctrine around to mean its direct opposite. James asks practical consequences to determine his truths and to determine them right now. He does not care about truths but only about practice; he does not care about practice as a *theory* of practice but only as concrete and forceful actions. And he thinks that a limited number of practical consequences are adequate for the determination of truths. It follows that success is borne out and justified by what is immediately successful, regardless of what may later prove to be its failures. But how are we to know what "works best" if we do not allow it to work indefinitely? Workability, like success, may

[8] *Pragmatism*, pp. 43–81.

support a certain theory in practice today and relinquish it, if not directly disprove it, tomorrow. But James evidently took no such difficulties into account.

That Peirce himself recognized the defection of James' pragmatism is evident in many passages of his essays, and since these make the contrast clearer we may cite several of them. Peirce says first of all that if pragmatism "really made Doing to be the Be-all and the End-all of life, that would be its death. For to say that we live for the mere sake of action, as action, regardless of the thought it carries out, would be to say that there is no such thing as rational purport." [4] There is this defense, however, to be made of James. He put his finger better than did Peirce, who was seeking for more valid and lasting contributions, upon the popular pulse, with the result that leading thinkers and literary men took up the term in its Jamesian meaning with avidity and seemed to discover in it the satisfaction of a palpable need.

What does it mean, in terms of the present work, to say that James' pragmatism was popularly accepted and that Peirce's was not? We must remember that the political doctrine in effect at the time was that of democracy, a democracy negatively considered and thought to rest upon irrational foundations. There is no inconsistency between a nominalistic ethics and a nominalistic interpretation of a political doctrine, between a pragmatic ethics of justification by immediate practicality and a *laissez faire* doctrine of liberalism. We must hasten to admit that in terms of the postulates which governed the day, James' victory over Peirce was demanded. James did exactly construct the ethics called for by negative democracy.

[4] *Collected Papers*, 5.429.

The Ethics of Charles S. Peirce

We have seen in the course of the book that another kind of interpretation is possible for democracy, that democratic principles are consistent with realism and with rationalism. If this is true, then Peirce's pragmatic theory of ethics will prove more consistent than James'. Positive democracy is consistent with the ethics of Peirce, and indeed demands it. In order to account for this consistency it will be necessary first to explain the ethics of Peirce. Peirce's argument will be set forth as nearly as possible in his own words.[5]

Quantitative treatment, and consequently continuity, is necessary for the advance of any science. Now, the theory of probability is simply the science of logic quantitatively treated, and the problem of probability is simply the general truth-falsity problem of logic. Probability is a continuous quantity, so that great advantages may be expected from this method of studying logic. Unfortunately, however, probability is the one branch of mathematics in which error in method and in results is common. This comes about because its fundamental principles are in dispute. We must therefore clarify the meaning of probability. The character of probability belongs to certain inferences. As Locke shows, when one man assents to what another man has proved, the foundation of his assent is the probability of the truth. But this does not mean that any tendency of the mind to acceptance is involved; it only means that, as Locke says, the probable argument is "such as for the most part carries truth with it."[6] Although the

[5] See Peirce, Chance, Love and Logic, Part I, Chap. 3.
[6] Essay Concerning Human Understanding, Bk. IV, Chap. 15, § 1.

absolute distinction between truth and falsity is the
reality, in the actual world it would involve a complete
sundering of the two. But the real fact which corre-
sponds to the probability is given in ultimately fixed
ratios of truth to falsity. With a few inferences of a
given kind, say ten or one hundred, considerable fluctua-
tion is shown, but when we come into the thousands
and millions, the fluctuations subside until the ratio
approximates closer and closer to a fixed limit. Probability, then, is defined as the proportion of true to false inferences of a given kind.

But there remains an important point to be discussed.
Since probability belongs to a given kind of inference
repeated indefinitely, what becomes of the individual
inference? It must be either true or false and can show
no probability; therefore in reference to a single inference
probability can have no meaning. Now, the number of
risks or inferences which a man draws in his whole life
is a finite one, and he cannot be absolutely certain that
the result will be in accord with the probabilities. Taking his risks collectively, it cannot be certain that they
will not fail. The case of the gambler and of the insurance company both illustrate the truth of this predicament. Given a finite number of instances, they
will profit, but in the long run, upon the indefinite
repetition of their operations, they must certainly fail.
But what is true of the insurance company is likewise
true of all other kinds of business. All human affairs
rest upon probabilities, and the same thing is true everywhere. If man were immortal he could be perfectly sure
of seeing the day when everything in which he had
trusted should betray his trust, and, in short, of coming
eventually to hopeless misery. He would break down,

at last, as every good fortune, as every dynasty, as every
civilization does. In place of this we have death.

But what, without death, would happen to every man,
with death must happen to some man. Death, however,
makes the number of risks or inferences finite and their
result uncertain. But since probability requires that this
number be indefinitely great, we are landed back in the
same difficulty, which seems to have but one solution.
We are driven to this, that logicality inexorably requires
that our interests shall not be limited. They must not
stop at our own fate, but must embrace the whole community. This community, again, must not be limited,
but must reach, however vaguely, beyond this geological
epoch, beyond all bounds. He who would not sacrifice
his own soul to save the whole world is illogical in all
his inferences collectively. So the social principle is
rooted in logic.

To be logical men should not be selfish; but they are
not in fact as selfish as they are thought. They speak
with anxiety of the exhaustion of coal in some hundreds
of years, or of the cooling-off of the sun in some millions. But it is not necessary for logicality that a man
should himself be capable of self-sacrifice. It is sufficient
that he recognizes the possibility of it and perceives that
only the inferences of that man who has it are really
logical, considering his own valid only in so far as they
would be accepted by the hero. This makes logicality
attainable enough. We cannot be strictly logical and
identify our interests with those of anything short of an
unlimited community. The soldier who runs to scale
a wall knows that he will probably be shot, but that is
not all he cares for. He also knows that if all the regi-
ment, with whom in feeling he identifies himself, rush

forward at once, the fort will be taken. Sometimes we can personally attain to heroism; in other cases we can only imitate the virtue. *But all this requires a conceived identification of one's interests with those of an unlimited community.*

The Positive Democratic Value of Peirce's Ethics

From a study of the theory of probability, Peirce has discovered implications which hold the possibility of far-reaching social consequences. The problem set in his remarkable argument is that of understanding the series of organizations, and the question—so important to humanity—of how the individual may identify his interests with it. What is involved is the issue of values. Peirce, himself, however, had a distinct aversion to, and an inability to cope with, the subject of value, as he readily admitted; and so he merely posed the problem, hinted at its solution, and left the deductions to be drawn by others. The importance of his achievement is not on this account to be underestimated.

Peirce's realistic philosophy led him to comprehend that the order of history is not the order called for by logic, yet he believed that history tends to approach logic, given a sufficiently great number of instances. There are symptoms here of Hegelianism but these are quickly dissipated by comparing Peirce's reasoning with the nominalistic conception of Hegel. Hegel maintained that history exhibits a certain fixed order (apprehensible in the past and present) which determines the course of events in the future. His reasoning thus led him to identify the course of history with the necessity of logic, or, in other words, to identify the historical order with the logical order; this was a completely nominalistic confusion. The identification of logic with the objects of knowledge yields an objective form of nominalism. A determinism of history is the consequence: the way things happen is the way they must happen. Karl Marx, in trying to make Hegel's dialectic actual, fell into this error. Marx's deduction of a materialistic dialectic is perfectly consistent, since it is frankly nominalistic, whereas Hegel's attempt to hold onto a halfway realism by somehow extrapolating the mind out into the objective world shows a lack of clarity which is even more indefensible.

Peirce, however, is careful to avoid this pitfall, and he warns many times against the confusion of psychology with logic. Logic is non-mental; but neither is it merely objective, as the theory of probability would at first glance lead us to believe. The number of instances which is required for probability to turn history into logic is not restricted and could easily be infinite. In fact in Peirce's version of pragmatism (the original pragmatism) it *is* infinite. Logic, and not the mind, is independent, operating equally on the knowing subject through the attempt of reasoning to grasp it, and on the objective world through the implicative course of events. The end-product of Hegel's reasoning is a determinism which inhibits initiative and hence action; the end-product of Marx's reasoning is the caution to lean on the vagaries of the dialectic; but the end-product of Peirce's reasoning is a direction which stimulates action toward a demonstrably desirable goal.

Human beings, like all other discrete identities, are at once finite and infinite. They endeavor to maintain their finite condition and yet to become one with all else in an infinite unity. Their existence as identities is dependent upon the limitations of finitude, and yet they strive to overcome this incompleteness and to merge with the totality of infinity. For human beings, there seem to be only two methods by which the striving toward this infinite goal is possible: through contemplation and through action. It is possible to seek *immediate* oneness with infinite unity only through the denial of finite existence, that is, through the pure contemplation of the infinite worth of the universe. This is the method chosen by the East; it is the way of the mystic. But there is another method. It is also possible to seek oneness with infinite unity by means of mediation, that is, by climbing the value series from smaller to greater organizations. In this method, one proceeds from the less inclusive to the more inclusive, towards the still more inclusive, with the goal of the utmost inclusive always in view. It is this latter method that the West has chosen, and the goal is the one that Peirce has described as the unlimited community.

Reason and the unlimited community are permanently identified, and with them is associated the love of life as lived in the vivid world of actuality. Reason requires that the road to the ideal of the unlimited community lie along the actual world. Only through society can the individual come upon this true meaning and purpose. Man exists for the sake of society, which in turn exists for the sake of the next higher value, and so on upwards until infinite value is reached. Through society, rational pursuits are enabled to advance. Each generation of scientists can start from the accomplishments of the generation before, and scientific knowledge becomes cumulative.

But Eastern mysticism knows nothing of this kind of

progress. The East teems with the denial of life, and offers a love of death and a perpetual nay-saying. Mystics are obliged to start afresh; they can neither build upon what has gone before nor pass on what they have discovered. "Let a man meditate on the syllable, Om," forever, as the Upanishads advise; yet he will have little in the way of communicable achievement to share with his fellows. Faith in transcendentalism, and indeed in irrationalisms of whatever sort, is equivalent to a lack of faith in the powers of reasoning and to a mistrust of the human situation. Thus it is plain that transcendental religion is opposed to the religious ideal of the unlimited community, which shares with Jesus Christ a belief in human destiny and the hope and promise of reason.

The necessity of the goal of the unlimited community as a guide to action is a truth which must reign supreme. Moreover, it is a truth which must remain true whether we are conscious of it or not. It is doubtful whether the human race could have survived, had not the impulses always been fundamentally rational. Men always act as though they feel that actuality does not exhaust existence. There have been few persons who have not at some time in their lives acted from narrowly selfish motives, and the great majority of persons do so most of the time. But let them not be deceived, says Peirce. There is a logic which governs discrete being, and it shall be only so much the worse for them if their actions prove contradictory. Those nominalists among us who accept the ultimate and exclusive reality of actuality would do well to consider the limited nature of all finite existence and the logic which prohibits possibility from being pre-empted by their experience.

There are those who believe in their own existence, because its opposite is inconceivable; yet the most balsamic
of all the sweets of sweet philosophy is the lesson that personal existence is an illusion and a practical joke. Those
that have loved themselves and not their neighbors will
find themselves April fools when the great April opens the
truth that neither selves nor neighborselves were anything
more than vicinities; while the love they would not en-
tertain was the essence of every scent.[7]

The point is that whether the individual is to live a
social life or not is never a question for the individual
to decide. He may or may not know that he exists to
serve society, but this is his purpose none the less, although it is true that he may fulfill it better when he is
made aware of it. However much we may fancy that we
feel, think and act as isolated and monadic individuals,
our actions are sure to have collective effects which must
rebound eventually upon the conditions of our individual
existence. This contention is clearly brought out in the
very study of the statistics of probability from which
Peirce deduced the goal of the unlimited community.

It is important to remember always, however, that
although on Peirce's ethical principle the individual
serves society and works thus toward a goal which lies
beyond his own narrow interests, this fact does not
preclude the value and validity of the individual at his
own peculiar level. There is such a thing as the importance of the individual which his function as part of
a social whole does not replace. The individual is both
part of a social whole and himself a whole to his own
parts, and, in terms of the latter consideration, what
serves his own intrinsic well-being is alone what matters.

[7] Peirce, Collected Papers, 4.68.

Yet the two ends are in no way conflicting; the individual can do justice to himself only by *not* setting himself up as a *final* end. Indeed, apart from the function of the individual as a contribution to society, it is difficult to see what the individual could mean. He is not an absolute isolate. None of us is self-sufficient in any complete sense, and it is only by making our own contribution to the social total, however small or large such an offering may be, that our individual selves are given concrete meaning.

We should by now be in a position to see that it is Peirce's ethics and not James' that we want for democracy. Peirce's ethical doctrine is consistent with positive democracy—more, it is demanded by it. The ethics of Peirce requires that the service of society be asked of the individual voluntarily upon his rational persuasion. The result must be a society of free men, rationally persuaded of the necessity for serving their common social goal. What could be more liberal and at the same time rational? Of course, it must be admitted that the difficulties in the way of the application of such an interpretation are great; but there is nothing which tells us that they are insuperable. The method of attaining such a rational liberal ethics for positive democracy is that of persuasion, which is to say education; its field of final accomplishment lies, perhaps, in a remote yet not indefinitely removed future; but its reward is sure to be that of a life of freedom and reason for the individual and of progress for society.

APPENDICES

Education and American Democracy

THE POSSIBILITY OF TRUE DEMOCRACY IS DEPENDENT UPON the acceptance of democratic principles on the part of the vast majority living within the state. This cannot be achieved by means of force but only by means of persuasion. Reasoning will persuade men into becoming adherents of democracy; clubbing will not. Education is a slow process but it is still the only one upon which persuasion is able to depend.

Neither of the opponents in the early struggle between American ideals was entirely triumphant. Hamilton represented the aristocracy of wealth and position. Jefferson stood not for a leveling democracy but rather for an aristocracy of ability, to be fostered by the state universities. But it was Andrew Jackson and his mob democracy which finally won out. Hamilton was hardly true to the American tradition, but both Jefferson and Jackson were. Unfortunately, Jackson's direct democracy, with its spoils system, triumphed over Jefferson's representative democracy. The American state universities have become one of the spoils; if they are not altogether political tools, then they serve as means for the indoctrination of what has been called the "mucker pose": the professed derogation of all avowed higher purposes.

The American emphasis on practicality, almost to the exclusion of theory, has deeply affected the state universities. The typical American community a century ago contained 25 vocations. The last national census counts 25,000. In the attempt to follow this trend, the universities have tried to turn themselves into trade schools. Abstract studies which do not provide any immediate practical application are derided, and everything from carpentry and cosmetics to radio-broadcasting is taught. The success of this policy is represented by enrollment. In the years from 1875 to 1903, the increased enrollment from 2,300 to 41,300 represents proportional ratios of population increase. But from 1903 to 1928 the enrollment increase to 183,000 represents business advantage. The universities have come to follow current trends; they make no attempt to lead them.

If the universities are "to teach a way of living rather than a way of making a living," as President Gilmore of the University of Iowa has remarked, the authority of the rational tradition over the intellectual life must be restored. Nominalism, which Mr. Norman Foerster [1] attacks under the better-known names of "scientism" and "naturalism," has been responsible for making man and the satisfaction of his material wants central, but has failed to take into account his reaction to the higher values. This bias, which has had such a disastrous effect on education, cannot be allowed to continue. The values which humanism champions should not suppress

[1] The American State University: Its Relation to Democracy (Chapel Hill, 1937).

those which are now dominant but must take precedence over them and lead them. "The key to educational reform is thus the college of liberal arts."

Mr. Foerster, who is Director of the School of Letters in the University of Iowa, is a prominent humanist. The attack of humanism upon the faults of the American universities is much the same as that of President Hutchins of the University of Chicago, who is a more pronounced rationalist. Mr. Foerster's book, however, consists largely of attack, and does not have the positive program that Dr. Hutchins offers. For instance, humanism leads Foerster to despair of the possibility of social science, whereas Hutchins wishes to make this one of the main features of his projected reform of the university.

Both Hutchins and Foerster see the task of the university as one of teaching what ought to be rather than what is, but Foerster goes on to make the fatal mistake of identifying humanism with what ought to be and naturalism with what is. This is wholly inconsistent with Foerster's later statement that "the central issue is whether we shall continue to regard man as merely a part of the flux of nature, or as, at the same time, *sui generis*." The independent values do not conflict with character but rather require it for recognition and the proper responses.

Mr. Foerster's book is good detailed criticism of the shortcomings we are now facing, but his solution of the difficulties is rather vague and indeterminate. On its negative side, humanism reveals very clearly the fact that it has much in common with realistic rationalism. Educational problems can only be resolved by the happy combination of rationalism with empiricism. Yet the humanists continue to be blinded to the fact that reasoning man is not something finally isolated, but is reacting to a world which everywhere exhibits a logical network of relations.

President Hutchins himself has written the most penetrating work upon the question of American universities.[2] Beginning with an attack upon the "empiricism" of the present trend toward the trade school kind of preparation for immediate practicality, he ends by expressing the desire that trade schools and what they teach, though important, should play no part in the university curriculum. Modern textbooks with their summary approach, and professors who are most proud of former successes in practical life, attempt to keep students informed of events, but only succeed in keeping them up with "event before last." Meanwhile education in reasoning—logic and mathematics—languishes.

Universities, he concludes, should teach only abstract principles, which can never become as old-fashioned as immediately practical techniques, and which therefore in the end prove the most practical. Hutchins calls for a return to the Greek ideal and to the mediaeval university, in both of which metaphysics is considered basic and knowledge a hierarchy. Accordingly, he would divide universities into three departments: metaphysics, and the natural and social sciences. After preparation in all three, with an emphasis on one, the student would then repair to a trade school in order to learn how to make a living.

The great significance of the problem which President Hutchins raises cannot be underestimated. The pragmatism which James advocated is more prevalent in

[2] *The Higher Learning in America* (New Haven, 1936).

America than anyone suspects, and has made a terrific impression upon the schools. What works is true; therefore let us teach workability and we shall also be teaching truth. The modern reduction of this error is exemplified in the statement by Heywood Broun, that he wished his son to learn something about the labor movement and not how to parse irregular Greek verbs. John Dewey, in a recent lecture, said that being ignorant of the (immediate) future, we should prepare our children for it! Such is the fallacy which reigns over American education. We have exchanged mediaeval rational dogmatism for a modern empirical dogmatism. The experimental sciences, though representing the best advance of recent times, threaten to swamp metaphysics and logic and the philosophical studies generally.

The result is that in a day when empiricism is alone considered the way to the discovery of truth, the teaching of truths already discovered is neglected, and abstract principles languish in favor of the laboratory. The contradiction in this position is obvious; it is easy to find students of science who are ignorant of scientific method; and, as we have seen, one investigator who made a tour of scientific laboratories throughout the United States reported that he could not find one single instance of theoretical science. Men who engage in this latter activity are scornfully termed "pencil scientists," and only laboratory work is valued. The answer is that American technology has advanced along all fronts, but there has been little American contribution to science.

Education analytically considered is of two kinds: (1) that which is concerned with the more remote future, and (2) that which is concerned with what Santayana calls the "dominant foreground." Corresponding with this distinction, there ought to be two kinds of educational institutions: (1) universities, and (2) trade schools. The universities would teach only the pure sciences and scientific method, logic, mathematics and metaphysics. The trade schools would teach applied science and technology, and the humbler trades. Rationality, as taught by the universities, would mean that the world is a non-contradictory and mutually implicative system of truths. As taught by the trade schools, it would mean that the world of actual practice is a dialectic, more or less blind, half rational, striving to attain to the conditions of complete rationality.

The function of universities should be to teach the truth and the methods of its discovery, in so far as this truth and these methods are known; nothing more. The university, as President Hutchins says, "is to provide a haven where the search for truth may go on unhampered by utility or pressure for 'results.'" The function of trade schools should be to achieve two ends: to teach the making of a living, and to teach how to make the making of a living a better and more rational affair; or, in other words, to teach students how to get along in the practical world, and also how to improve the accepted practice in accordance with the truth taught in the universities. Thus the unity of theory and practice would be taught theoretically in the university, demonstrated in the trade school, and practiced in the world of affairs.

Nowhere else has the prevailing world-philosophy of nominalism had so devastating an effect as in America. The sole reality of the actual physical world has cruelly confined the American to the narrow compass of his own senses. That this set of ideas must penetrate to the universities and do great damage there in the way of limiting speculative thought, is to have been expected. Hutchins is protesting against the continuance of this erroneous philosophy as it is implicitly accepted in education. He wishes to substitute for it a realism which acknowledges the validity of metaphysics, retained not only in such studies as logic and mathematics but also in the principles and method of the abstract sciences. He believes, in other words, that the only way to brilliant inductive insight lies through a thorough familiarity with deductive systems. Since it is never known what are the particular practical problems with which students will be confronted, the surest way to help them is to instruct them theoretically in the abstract solving of problems.

President Hutchins is sincere; he is also intelligent and fearless. He wishes to restore the universities to their ancient and honorable prestige, and finds that such a task requires a return to the supremacy of metaphysics. Frequently he commits serious blunders himself, as in the hiring of Rudolf Carnap, whose anti-metaphysical positivism is squarely opposed to all the ideals for which Hutchins has fought. But his strength lies in the fact that his position is fundamentally the correct one and his reforms urgently necessary. President Hutchins stands out indeed in a wilderness of fact-finding scientists and metaphysics-shy philosophers as one of the hopes of American educational life.

APPENDIX II

Democracy in England

THE MORE THAT VARIOUS CONTEMPORARY DEMOCRACIES
are studied the more it becomes clear that the basic
problems which all are facing are essentially the same.
There are various minor differences of course, but since
the governments of England, France and the United
States, for instance, share a common political and a
common economic system, and since the internal threat
to democracy today comes from the economic sphere,
it is not strange that the problem of the preservation of
democracy should be the same in each country.

The government of England is the outstanding example of the democratic experiment in our time. It is
the oldest democracy, and it has been the most firmly
established. For this reason its citizens have proved
individually to be the most amenable to reason and have
grown to accept the democratic principles as a matter
of course. Certainly to have abided for so long by an
unwritten constitution is evidence of an understanding
of democracy and an allegiance to it which is perhaps
unparalleled in history. "There is not," says Laski, "and
there never has been, in our system any body of fundamental rights, either explicit or implied, that are safe
from change by the direct will of Parliament." [1] This,

[1] *Parliamentary Government*, p. 106.

in its complete application, would be the nearest to what is meant by government by reason: the government of the majority together with the protection from outrage of minority rights, giving rise to the preservation of fundamental liberties.

No English party has remained in office for more than ten years since 1832, a good example of the oscillation in power so necessary to the operation of democracy. It is interesting to inquire what such an alternation of state power between parties has rested on, especially in these days when the gaining of control by any party in a democracy tends to become permanent and, by outlawing the party or parties not in power, to disrupt and perhaps destroy the party system. We have Mr. Laski's word for it that the success of democracy in England rested upon a fundamental agreement between parties, at least as to the economic basis upon which the government was founded. No one raised the question of the economic nature of the English democracy, and the mock warfare of the parties did not ever turn up those urgent questions of the ownership of economic control and its effect upon government which are so dangerous to the democratic form. "The explanation surely is that they [the political parties] all agreed about the framework within which they were to operate; and the society of which that framework was the expression was rich enough and elastic enough to permit ample margins within which discussion of differences could be at once permitted and lead to acceptable compromises. For invariably, the framework itself was not brought into discussion." [2] The economic system of capitalism is of course the framework in question.

[2] Ibid., p. 95.

The successful operation of party government in England has been due to the fact that there have never been two parties. There has been only one party with two wings. The issues which the parties have quarreled over have been relatively trivial. And just as the disagreement of parties over fundamentals is apt to wreck the democratic system, so the complete agreement between parties is apt to do away with it. There is apparently a very precise compromise, an extremely nice level, of agreement, defection from which on either side spells the end of democratic government. Too complete an agreement between parties leads to a one-party-with-two-wings system, with its stagnation and opposition to all important change. Too radical a disagreement between parties means disagreement over economic fundamentals where victory by either party is likely to lead to the enforced dissolution of the other—and either to violent change or to violent opposition to all change. England's error, if any, in this respect has been that of too complete agreement between parties. It has been nearly impossible sometimes to tell which wing of the Conservative party—for that is a name which in a sense we may also give to the Liberals—was actually administering to the requirements of actual government, and which was out of power.

Now, however, the situation is entirely different. In England, as in other democracies, capitalism has reached the stage where a contracting economy has forced it to retrench, and when this happens "doubt is raised whether parliamentary institutions are any more appropriate to the expression of capitalism." [3] The competing groups have come to be represented by the Conservative party

[3] *Ibid.*, p. 204.

and the Labour party, each of which stands for an inflexible program. The first offers the maintenance of the economic *status quo* while the other promises the socialization of industry. The Conservative party is at present in power; but in power or out, the Conservatives have tremendous influences on their side. The House of Lords is almost a solid Conservative body, with power to delay for two years any legislation emanating from the House of Commons. The British Civil Service is predominantly Conservative, as for the most part is also the Judiciary. Whether these groups would allow the Labour party, if it ever does succeed in attaining power, to go through peacefully and democratically with its program of reform is the vital question. For in England, too, liberal democracy is threatened by the class struggle.

In America it has been the judiciary which has served as the conservative organ blocking the advance of reform legislature. But in England no document stands between the elected members of the House of Commons and the execution of their will. The difficulty is of another sort. The American liberals who are eager to turn over to the President more and more executive power would do well to learn something from the English example. For the increase of executive power is all very well, when the President in office is a liberal like Roosevelt. But when he is a Conservative of the stamp of Chamberlain, the result is quite different; and who knows the aims of Roosevelt's successor? The threat to democracy in England very definitely arises from the influences that determine the control which the Prime Minister exercises. The Cabinet takes orders, as more and more of their duties are usurped by the Prime Minister. For instance it is well known that Chamberlain is to a large extent his own foreign minister. And the House of Commons has become a rubber stamp for the execution of the Prime Minister's designs.

The democracy of England, like that of the United States and France, is in unmistakable crisis. Capitalism is doomed. What the Webbs have termed the "inevitability of gradualness" is working upon it. Some kind of socialized democracy is certain, if democracy is to survive at all. "But working to a Socialist society through the parliamentary system does not merely mean that the Standing Orders and the conventions of the Constitution are observed. It means also that business men who have no confidence in the new order will yet so restrain themselves as to act as though they have." [4] This on the face of it seems extremely unlikely. Yet what are the alternatives? Fascism—or civil war: the pattern followed by Germany or by Spain. The prospect seems too horrible to contemplate, but the issue is definitely one which has got to be decided. Can democracy in England survive the decision? The question at issue is only whether conservative leadership conducts toward a clear and sharp end of capitalism (socialized democracy) or a confused and rough one (fascism). At any rate the case for democracy is what is to be tried: is a whole-hearted democracy wanted, or none at all?

[4] *Ibid.*, p. 188.

Democracy in France

WHEN WE COME TO EXAMINE ACTUAL DEMOCRACIES WE notice an astonishing similarity prevailing among the conditions in different countries. It is not a coincidence that simultaneously with the assailing of democracy upon all sides the democratic governments have been experiencing internal crises. As democracy is challenged in Britain and the United States, so it is also challenged in France.

In France as in other countries the attack is based upon the superiority of dictatorships—their greater concentration, unity, mobility, etc. But none of the arguments bear up under an examination. As R.E. Lacombe has shown, the dictatorships suffer from the same difficulties that plague the democracies; they do not provide the proper remedy.[1] Is it better to act quickly or to act correctly? Is it better to have a seeming unanimity of opinion and allegiance or an honestly and openly expressed difference?

Of representative government we are told now and again that its elected representatives are also its host of dictators: "France has given itself six hundred tyrants who prosper as dependents of the State"; but, replies La-

[1] "*Les vices de la démocratie et leurs remedès,*" *Revue de Métaphysique et de Morale,* July, 1938.

combe to this criticism, the single autocratic tyrant rules through the intermediation of a multitude of subordinate tyrants, who are no less merciless and bureaucratic. It is, for instance, a well known fact that the administrators of fascism in Italy after so many years of Mussolini's rule constitute almost a class by themselves, a vested bureaucracy which it would be almost impossible to shake loose without resorting to an invasion. Another common criticism of democracy in France, according to Lacombe, is that which is directed against the party system. Measures which do not interest the great parties do not get enacted into law. But then do they under fascism? No, clearly dictatorship is not "streamlined democracy"; it is not democracy at all. Despite the many weaknesses of democracy, it is better than dictatorship, which does nothing to correct those weaknesses, but either substitutes other shortcomings which are worse or retains the old ones.

The peculiar difficulty with French democracy is the short tenure in office of the premier and the cabinet. Lacombe says that they are supposed to fall every three years, but they seldom last three months. This is an inherent constitutional difficulty. But there exist others, of a more immediate and practical kind which would be perhaps even harder to remedy. The danger to democracy, to which in an earlier chapter we gave warning,[2] of the incursion of the class struggle into the platforms of the leading political parties, has actually occurred in France. The political struggle for power in French democracy, which has now assumed rigid class lines, is likely to disrupt the very form of democratic government. The struggle is too bitter, and that fundamental

[2] Chapter X.

ground of agreement, according to which the parties allow each other to alternate in power, is missing. There is no incentive to either party to relinquish control merely in order to be consistent with a form of government when neither side believes that the other will sincerely allow it to remain.

The result is a struggle to the death. There is a strike of labor, and this is countered with a strike of capital. Labor unwillingly co-operates with a government initiated by the so-called ruling six hundred families; and when the "*front populaire*" government takes over, the financiers refuse to lend it any funds. The stalemate which ensues proves that neither class is strong enough at present to render the outcome a decisive one. But that does not mean that the democracy functions effectively in the meanwhile. For the stalemate almost allows France to operate without any effective government,—or with the kind of coalition government that Daladier represents, in which nobody believes. Such a neutrality built not upon a fundamental agreement but upon countervailing forces makes France vulnerable from the outside; she is powerless to interfere in what any other nation does or does not do; and she ceases to be a world power. This is not the triumph of democratic government but rather its eclipse.

The misfortunes of French democracy are not only the misfortunes of France; they are also the misfortunes of democracy. They are indicative of an increasing movement of failure among the democracies. But from what does the failure of democracy result? Not from the innately contradictory nature of democracy, but only from the way in which everywhere today it has been put into effect. The essence of democracy consists in allow-

ing the citizens to decide the affairs of the state. But
what is to help the citizens make such decisions? Nothing but chance prejudice and caprice, or at best economic
interest? These occasions have their merits. A democracy would be inconceivable in which some decisions
were not left to the arbitrary choice of the citizens, and
in which the citizens were not ruled strongly by economic interest. But without other criteria, the result
must be precisely what exists in France today. Something more is required, and that something is the authority of reason which must in turn rule the citizens.
Not authority ruling in the name of reason—we have had
enough of that. But reason as a new approach to education could impart it to citizens: the sole authority of
the notion of justice, which is reason in government.
This force, and this alone can save positive democracy
in France. An equable state can result only if the state
ceases to be merely the "field of the struggle of individual
interests" and if each citizen has at heart, besides his
own welfare, the welfare of the whole population; if, in
short, he understands that he cannot hope to prosper in
a community which is alien to prosperity. French democracy is old among modern democracies, but no one
of the contemporary democracies is old as nations go.
We must refurbish democracy with reason and give it
a positive cast if it is to survive and become more and
more that which we had hoped it would be.

Prospects

of the Survival of Democratic Principles

in Socialism

IT IS ALL BUT IMPOSSIBLE TO GET AT THE TRUTH OF WHAT is happening in Soviet Russia. There are two reasons for this. In the first place, personal accounts are usually colored by extreme prejudices. Travelers to Russia either despise what the communists are doing so much that they can see no good in it, or they worship it and therefore remain blind to its shortcomings. In the second place, the country itself is so vast and the changes which are taking place in every walk of life are occurring so rapidly that even an impartial and painstaking observer with the best will in the world would have trouble in coming to a conclusion concerning any distinct phase of Soviet activity. Thus in attempting to answer the question in which advocates of democracy manifest the most interest, namely, whether democratic principles have survived in the socialism which Soviet Russia is endeavoring to put into effect, we are handicapped to the point where no decisive answer can be given.

We shall have to do the best we can. Our method will be to ignore the many travel books which have described conditions prevailing in Russia, on the plea that the rate of change of social conditions would appear to be such as to render books of this sort outmoded before they are placed on the counters. Although nothing in Russia seems to hold for very long, we can probably get the best survey of the problem in which we are interested by examining the avowed program of the communists, in the writings of the Marxists and the Soviet economists. If this will not tell us where the communists of Soviet Russia are at present, at least it will give us some indication of where they hope to go, and that is perhaps as good an index as any.

The communists hope first to replace a dictatorship of the capitalists by a dictatorship of the proletariat. The control of democracies, they say, has been taken over by finance capital, and thus, identifying logically whatever occurs together historically, they have no use for democracy, regarding it as an inevitable instrument of capitalism. And indeed, they do not seek to supplant the present democracies with a better—at least not right away. They seek to substitute one dictatorship for another, to put the class of the worker in place of the class of the owner. Democratic equality on an economic level is sought soon enough; but democratic equality on a political level is postponed until the dictatorship of the proletariat has restored the balance upset by the previous dictatorship of the capitalists, and a classless society predicated upon the consequent withering away of the state, can be established. This classless society presumably will add a political equality to the economic equality sought at present. Finally, genuine democracy will be established.

The program is all to the good. But in the meanwhile is it true that economic equality has actually been established? No one knows. Certainly the vast majority of the farmers and agricultural workers have benefited, but what of the urban dwellers? Have the ruling Soviets replaced with privileges of use the power of possessions which was the pride of the previous nobility? Is there what we might call not political but economic freedom: the right to strike, to change jobs, to complain of conditions in a factory? Again, no one knows.

There is one political gain that we do know about. This is the substitution of functional for geographical representation in the Soviets.[1] Political representation issues from divisions of labor rather than from locations of residence, by all odds a more democratic criterion, since it is what the citizen contributes to the common social welfare and not where he happens to live that matters the most in his relations to the state. That is a gain; but what of the rest of the liberties of political democracy? Is the Soviet citizen free to criticize Stalin in public? Is he free to form an opposition party?[2] Is he free to print a book devoted to the alternatives to communism in

[1] A good brief account of the machinery of functional representation is offered by Joad in his Guide to the Philosophy of Morals and Politics, p. 749.

[2] Communists insist that since parties are founded on economic differences there is no reason for them to exist in a state where capitalism has been liquidated, but this is not true. Many reasons can be found for the existence of parties other than economic differences. It would be theoretically possible, for example, to have two political parties in Russia both agreed as to the economic framework but differing, let us say, as to policy in foreign relations, as to the rate of industrialization and consequent sacrifice of the present generation, and so forth.

which one of the alternatives is made to appear in a better light? Is he, in fact, free to oppose the existing regime in any form but that of private thought? Perhaps; but probably not.

The revolution which Russia has undergone is not considered, so to speak, to have ended the Revolution in Russia. True democracy is still a long way off, if indeed it ever comes. "Thus, before the revolutionary period pure democracy is found to be inoperative, and during the revolutionary period it is declared to be impracticable. Until the revolution is accomplished, it is upon the militant resolution and energy of will of the few, rather than upon the possibility of obtaining universal consent, that communists rely in the struggle against Capitalism." [3] The few always speak in the name of the masses; and they are doing so again. But it is questionable indeed whether the advance guard of the proletariat will in the future voluntarily relinquish state power any more willingly and freely than the capitalists do at the present time.

The only explanation which permits us to view events in Russia in a favorable light from the point of view of political democracy is the one which holds that Soviet Russia is at present in a state of war, a war with the surrounding capitalistic nations. It must arm, it must ceaselessly hunt down *saboteurs*, and it must defend itself from within by temporarily suspending the civil liberties in order the better to defend itself from without, much in the manner of the democratic countries during the World War of 1914. According to this explanation, as soon as Soviet Russia no longer needs to fear invasion or disruption of its program from without, the barriers

[3] Joad, op. cit., p. 692.

in the way of free speech, free assembly and freedom of the press will be let down, and political democracy will take its rightful place next to economic democracy.

There are two pieces of evidence in favor of this view. The first is that it seems to correspond closely with the actual situation. Certainly Soviet Russia is ringed with enemies, and if the speeches of neighboring dictators are anything to the purpose, invasion is never far distant. Japan, Germany, also England and the Catholic Church, each have their own reasons for desiring the downfall of the stronghold of communism. If Soviet Russia is to retain its present form of government it must be vigilant even at the current expense of the exercise of civil liberties.

The second piece of evidence is contained in the New Soviet Constitution which was adopted in 1937. Article 125 of the Constitution reads as follows:

> In conformity with the interests of the toilers, and in order to strengthen the socialist system, the citizens of the U.S.S.R. are guaranteed:
> a. Freedom of speech;
> b. Freedom of the press;
> c. Freedom of assembly and of holding mass meetings;
> d. Freedom of street processions and demonstrations.
> These rights of the citizens are ensured by placing at the disposal of the toilers and their organizations printing presses, supplies of paper, public buildings, the streets, means of communication and other material requisites for the exercise of these rights.

Added to this is Article 118, the right to work, 119, the right to rest and leisure, 120, sickness and old age maintenance, 121, the right to education,[4] 122, the absolute

[4] According to Article 124, "Freedom of religious worship and freedom of anti-religious propaganda are recognized for all citizens," but

equality of rights of women, 123, the absolute equality
of rights of citizens, etc. The whole of Chapter X com-
prising "The Fundamental Rights and Duties of Citizens" is as liberal a document as has ever been executed
and formally adopted.

Now, of course, the major part of the political tenets
of liberalism contained in this Constitution have never
been actually put into effect. Any citizen who demanded of the government a printing press and supply
of paper in order to exercise the freedom of the press by
publishing an attack upon the eligibility of Comrade
Stalin to continue as Secretary of the Party would be, to
put it mildly, discouraged in a way which would probably
prevent him from ever making the experiment again.
But, as we began by saying, the question is not what the
actual conditions are in Russia today; they change too
fast to be indicative of anything. We are rather interested in trends, in determining which way the Soviet
communists are driving. If in the midst of their present
difficulties and dangers they have chosen to adopt an
extremely liberal constitution, it must be because they
have set themselves such a goal. If they actually succeed
in attaining to it, if it ever becomes a part of the life of
Soviet Russia, we may expect that Soviet Russia will be
more liberal than any government in the world today.

More liberal; we cannot say more democratic, since
unfortunately there is no provision for the party system
whereby an opposition can make itself heard legally and
peacefully. There is majority rule, but no such thing

freedom of religious instruction is conspicuous by its absence. Is not
the study of comparative religions, at least, a matter of education? The
young citizen can learn about all religions and then, if there exist the
freedoms mentioned above, choose either one of the religions he has
been taught—or none, as his reason dictates.

as majority rule "having regard for the rights of the minority." It is from the protection of minority rights that the logical issue of liberal principles is made applicable to all. The liberal tenets are a matter of fiat and do not stem from the protection of minority rights as a source. Thus in a sense there is no democracy planned. There is only liberalism, artificially provided for. The omission is probably due to the fact that communists identify minority rights with the property rights of capitalists, but this is far from being its only or necessary meaning. The protection of minority rights need not apply at the economic level at all, but only at the political. Parties can exist for the purpose of choosing between the candidates for high office on a basis of their fitness; they can be for the choice between various foreign and domestic policies, and so on, all without touching upon the question of the fundamental economic framework of the socialist society.

In conclusion, therefore, it would appear that while there is little at present either of liberalism or democracy practiced in Soviet Russia, liberalism has been planned but democracy has not. In Russia as in other socialist states, however, it would be possible to have democracy as well as liberalism without in any way sacrificing the economic foundations of socialism, which in fact would provide the only example of democracy at the economic level which has ever been put into effect. Democracy has not survived in socialism; but its revival by socialism would be logical. And, finally, the survival of democratic principles in socialism, on a scale never hitherto envisaged, and with the addition of political liberties, economic rights, and the democratic party system, is entirely possible.

Index

Absolute law, as goal, 160
Absolute truth exists, 67
Activity, as end, 215
Adler, Mortimer J., 140 f.
Alternation in office, 235
Ambrose, 26
American Indian, 84
American labor in politics, 173
American life, and technology, 197
American parties, and class divisions, 179; as economic divisions, 171 f.
American practice, and European theory, 198
American Revolution, as class struggle, 182
American theory, dearth of, 199; need for, 200
Anarchy, and liberalism, 163; function of, 163
Animistic culture, 85; and communal life, 90; and individual, 89 f.
Aquinas, Thomas, 20, 26, 95
Aristotle, 5, 26, 45, 65
Ascoli, Max, 185
Assyria, ancient, 86, 93
Athens, 102
Authority as coercion, 35

Babylonians, 102
Bacon, 108
Bagehot, 27
Basil, 26
Beard, Charles A., 173
Belief, failure of, 155; in science, 120; levels of, 119; not always conscious, 118

Bentham, 25, 152, 158, 164
Berengar, 114
Blackstone, 23
Boethius, 5
Boyle, Robert, 116
Bridgman, P. W., 104 ff., 114
Broun, Heywood, 231
Bryan, W. J., 172
Burke, Thomas, 27
Burtt, E. A., 114
Butler, Bishop Joseph, 24, 29

Cairns, Huntington, 23, 25 f., 45
Capella, 5
Capitalism, and democracy, 28; decline of, 28
Carnap, Rudolf, 233
Carrel, Alexis, 111 f.
Cause, and occasion, 3
Cervantes, 89
Character, defined, 147; nature of, 146
Civilization, and primitive organization, 102
Class struggle, and democracy, 179. See also American Revolution
Cohen, M. R., 106 f.
Coke, 23
Collectivism. See Individualism
Communism and dialectical materialism, 65
Comte, Auguste, 85
Contract and use, 25
Conze, Edward, mentioned, 6, 8; quoted, 4 f.
Copernicus, 116
Crowther, J. G., 205 f.
Culture, and dominant ontology, 88; as applied philosophy, 83;

251

www.ingramcontent.com/pod-product-compliance
Lightning Source LLC
Chambersburg PA
CBHW021812270326
41932CB00007B/149